Tao Te Ch

道德經

Lao Tzu, legendary writer of the Tao Te Ching, leaves China on a water buffalo. Chinese bronze figure from the 17th century. On the previous page is a Chinese woodcut with the same motif.

Tao Te Ching

The Taoism of Lao Tzu Explained

Stefan Stenudd

Stefan Stenudd is a Swedish author, artist, and historian of ideas. He has published a number of books in Swedish as well as English, both fiction and non-fiction. Among the latter are books about Taoism, the cosmology of the Greek philosophers, the Japanese martial arts, life force concepts, and astrology.

His novels explore existential subjects in settings from stoneage drama to science fiction, but lately stay more and more focused on the present. He has written some plays for the stage and the screen. In the history of ideas he studies the thought patterns of creation myths, but also Aristotle's Poetics. He is an aikido instructor, 6 dan Aikikai Shihan, Vice Chairman of the International Aikido Federation, member of the Swedish Aikido Grading Committee, and President of the Swedish Budo & Martial Arts Federation. He has his own extensive website:
www.stenudd.com

Also by Stefan Stenudd:
Cosmos of the Ancients: The Greek Philosophers on Myth and Cosmology, 2007.
Life Energy Encyclopedia, 2009.
Qi: Increase Your Life Energy, 2008.
Aikido Principles, 2008.
Attacks in Aikido, 2008.
Aikibatto: Sword Exercises for Aikido Students, 2007.
Your Health in Your Horoscope, 2009.
All's End, 2007.
Murder, 2006.

Stefan Stenudd's Taoism Website:
www.taoistic.com

Tao Te Ching: The Taoism of Lao Tzu Explained.
Copyright © Stefan Stenudd, 2011
Book design by the author.
All rights reserved.
ISBN: 978-91-7894-039-4
Publisher: Arriba, Malmö, Sweden, info@arriba.se
www.arriba.se

Contents

Preface 7
Introduction 13

Tao, the Way

1 It's All Real 37
2 Don't Split the Unity 40
3 As Little as Possible 46
4 The Hidden Cause 49
5 The Limit of Compassion 53
6 The Womb 57
7 Unselfishness 59
8 Good 61
9 Moderation in All 67
10 Modest Omnipotence 71
11 The Necessity of Emptiness 76
12 Moderation 79
13 Fear 82
14 Obscure Tao 86
15 Ancient Excellence 88
16 The Cycle of Life 91
17 Unnoticed Ruler 94
18 Pretense 97
19 Gain by Abandoning 100
20 I Am Alone 104
21 The Clarity of Obscurity 111
22 Humility Brings Honor 116
23 Deprived of Deprivation 119
24 Banned If You Boast 121
25 Four Greats 123
26 Be Still 127
27 Teacher and Student 129
28 Be Like Uncarved Wood 132
29 Don't Change the World 137
30 Peaceful Solutions 141
31 Victory Is Cause for Grief 144
32 All Follow Those Who Follow Tao 147
33 Longevity 150
34 It's Great to Be Small 154
35 Elusive, But Never Exhausted 157
36 One Postulates the Other 159
37 Nameless Simplicity 163

Te, the Virtue

38 The Highest Virtue 169
39 Unity with the One 174
40 A Cyclic Universe 177
41 Laughing Out Loud 179
42 Violence Meets a Violent End 182
43 Non-Action 187
44 Life Is the Treasure 189
45 Appearances 191
46 Enough Is Enough 194
47 Understanding without Exploring 196
48 Let Go 199
49 The Concern of the Sage 202
50 How to Survive 204
51 All Things Are Nurtured 207
52 Return to Clarity 210
53 Robbery 214
54 Cultivate Virtue 216
55 The Virtue of the Infant 219
56 Integrity 223
57 People Can Govern Themselves 226

58 What to Trust? 229
59 Rule with Moderation 232
60 The Ghosts Approve 235
61 Conquer by Yielding 237
62 The Greatest Gift 240
63 Big Is Small at First 242
64 The Sage Dares Not Act 245
65 No Rule by Knowledge 250
66 Go Low to Stand High 254
67 Battle with Compassion 257
68 Peaceful Warriors 261
69 Like a Guest 264
70 Easy to Understand 267

71 Knowing Illness 270
72 Don't Make Them Weary 272
73 Heaven's Way 275
74 The Supreme Executioner 280
75 People versus Rulers 284
76 Life Is Soft and Weak 287
77 Raise the Low 289
78 Water Surpasses All 291
79 Honor the Settlement 295
80 Simple Utopia 299
81 The Ideal 302

Literature 309

Preface

My first meeting with the *Tao Te Ching* was in my late teens. It was Toshikazu Ichimura, my Japanese teacher of the peaceful martial art aikido, who gave me a copy of it – the Gia-Fu Feng and Jane English version with beautiful calligraphy, which is still in print. He thought that my impatiently inquisitive mind would benefit from studying it.

Already by reading the first chapter, which compares desire and the freedom from desire without seeming judgmental, I was hooked. That appeals to a teenager.

The book remained with me, far beyond my teen years. It spoke of so many other things that I found relevant. Contrary to most reading experiences of my youth, I found Lao Tzu's work to increase its relevance, as if written in a future that we still have not reached. That alone is an enigma making it impossible to let the book gather dust in the shelf. It contains many others.

Tao Te Ching, which is the major source of Taoism, has a clouded origin. It was composed no earlier than the 6th and no later than the 4th century BC. According to legend, its writer was Lao Tzu, a high official of the Chinese empire, who left his work and his country in dismay, fed up with the charade of government.

He is said to have departed riding on a water buffalo. A border guard, impressed by his wisdom, pleaded him to write down his thoughts before leaving China. So he did. Then he crossed the border, never to be seen again.

His text is around five thousand words long, divided into two parts. One of them begins with the word *Tao*, the Way, the other with the word *Te*, virtue. The *Tao Te Ching*, the Book on the Way and Virtue, is a text as difficult to interpret as its origin is to ascertain. It speaks with simple directness, but conveys ideas so elusive that they have been discussed for over two thousand years, without any consensus reached as to their meaning.

Although clear about presenting a worldview and arguing for it, the book is written with the elegance and artistry that makes it most appropriate to call it a poem. Also, most of it is rhymed. That's not very difficult with Chinese rules for rhyme, but it still indicates that the author intended more than to pursue a line of reasoning.

Probably, the subtleties included were only possible to put into words with the added sophistication of poetry. What was to be said needed an artistic approach, just like some complex truths about the conditions of life need fiction to be pointed out.

To be understood at all, the text needs to be contemplated and interpreted by several minds. This has indeed been done, through the centuries, and that process is not at all slowing down.

Tao Te Ching has had countless Chinese commentaries through its circa 2,500 years of existence. The text reached the West rather late, but we've more than made up for that by an accelerating number of Western translations in the last hundred years. They keep coming.

That's necessary. The text is far too vague and unclear to be trusted to just one translation. There must be several perspectives in which to see it and several shapes in which to form its wordings in English and other languages.

No doubt, although the text has been kept faithfully intact through all this time, each generation needs its renewed interpretations in order to approach it and grasp its subtle meaning.

That's true for any classic. In a constantly changing world, it's necessary to reinterpret the classics in order to have a chance of grasping them. That way, we may even succeed to reveal new things about them, and come closer to a definitive understanding of them. Even if we don't, it's by reexamination that we keep them alive and carry them with us into the future. The words of Lao Tzu definitely belong to those that deserve our continued attention and preservation.

So, here is my version of the *Tao Te Ching*.

Almost twenty years ago, I made a Swedish translation of Lao Tzu's text, the first edition of which was published in 1992. Actually, the project started with another goal in mind.

In the 1980's, I was writing a novel and got the idea to begin each chapter with a quote from the *Tao Te Ching*. That would fit my story in an intriguing way. But the few existing Swedish versions of the Chinese classic didn't appeal to me as much as the English versions I had come across. After some struggle, I came to the conclusion that I needed to make my own translations of the quotes I wanted to use.

The job was mesmerizing, so I found myself translating the whole book. I was still in doubt about it, until a prominent Chinese poet, Li Li, who lives in Sweden, agreed to proof read. He approved of my version, with some kind words about it that made me confident enough to have it published. My novel was published later the same year.

Since then, I have reexamined and reworked my Swedish version of the *Tao Te Ching* in several editions. It has become an obsession.

For this English edition, though, I started all over. I wanted to avoid following old trains of thought and any

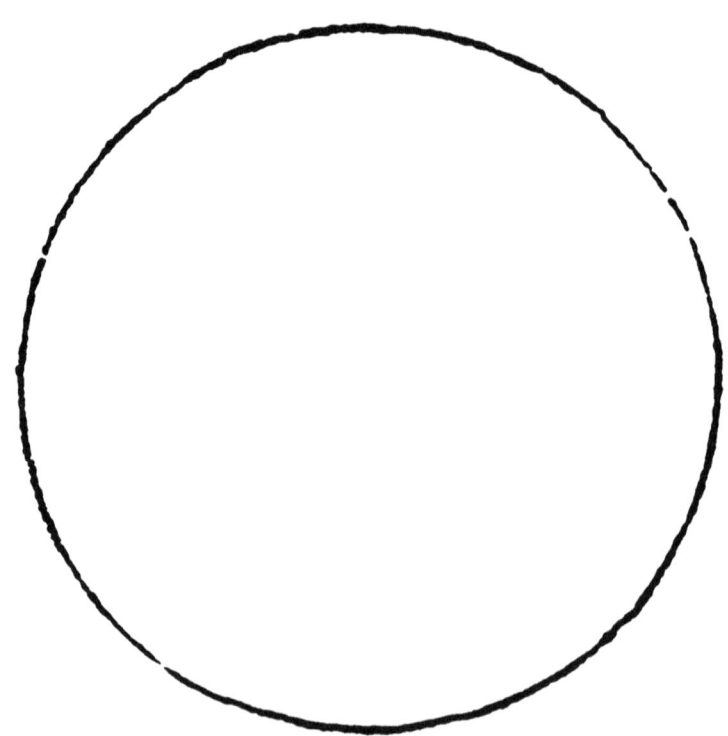

T'a Chi, the Supreme Origin. Symbol of the foundation of the world. It is most often represented by the well-known yin and yang symbol. Chinese illustration from the 18th century.

preconceptions. The translation into another language needed a fresh approach.

Sure enough, it made me discover new things about the text and coming to new conclusions about its content. So, for me it was again a wonderful journey. I hope the reader will share some of my delight.

In this version, I have returned to a very old tradition in dealing with the classics, practiced in the East as well as in the West. I let each chapter be followed by my comments about it. That way, the reader will have me as a close companion all through the *Tao Te Ching*. Those who prefer to do the voyage through Lao Tzu's words all by themselves can simply skip my comments and go directly from chapter to chapter of the translated text.

As for my comments, I mainly try to explain what I believe Lao Tzu to be pointing out in each chapter. I frequently use modern phenomena as references, so that it's obvious how much Lao Tzu still has to teach us. I have no doubt of it.

Where needed, I also explain some circumstances of the Chinese context in which Lao Tzu was writing. But most of his text deals with matters that are just as true now, in the Western world, as they were in China some 2,500 years ago.

As for my translation of the *Tao Te Ching* chapters, my main effort has been to make the text direct, to the point, without additional poetic clouding or any attempt of decorating it in a manner common for sacred texts. That's how I perceive the original.

Lao Tzu spoke with amazing simplicity and clarity, using almost no decorations or other intricacies in his language. Although the meaning behind them is often vague, maybe even cryptic, his words are easy to understand.

That's what I have tried to accomplish in this translation. Lao Tzu's message is far too important for his words to be covered in archaic artistry that was not present to begin with.

Like many other supreme works of literature, his words remain here and now, no matter how many years have passed since they were written. In translating them, we should not try to cover them in dust, as a futile method of dating them, but brush them off and present them in the purity and relevance they seem never to lose.

Tao Te Ching is one of those books that forever stay contemporary.

Stefan Senudd
February, 2011

Introduction

Tao Te Ching, the Book on the Way and Virtue, has an unclear origin in ancient China. It is said to be written by Lao Tzu, a public servant of some dignity in the court of the emperor, but it's not ascertained that he ever existed.

Legend has it that he was an older contemporary of K'ung Tzu, Confucius, who lived 551 to 479 BC, and whose existence is well documented in historical sources. The life of Lao Tzu, on the other hand, was not explicitly recorded until *Shih chi*, the book of Chinese history written by Ssu-ma Ch'ien around 90 BC. He even describes a meeting between Lao Tzu and K'ung Tzu, where the former is portrayed as both older and wiser, giving the latter a lesson that is almost humiliating.

Old Master

Age equaled wisdom and superiority in ancient China, and Confucianism was the leading philosophy already soon after the death of its creator, so Taoists would have wished for Lao Tzu to be the senior of the two. Thereby, his thoughts would gain the prestige of being of older origin.

Taoism and Confucianism are sort of competing philosophies, largely opposites of each another. Where Confucianism preaches obedience and strict conformity to social rules and human authorities, Taoism is almost indifferent to formalized social order. Instead, it advocates the return to a natural state of things, where the emperor and the farmer must be equally yielding and hesitant to spring into action.

Also, Lao Tzu got his philosophy from how he believed the whole world had emerged, in the beginning of time and in accordance with the principle of Tao, the Way. To him, the

Lao Tzu. Ink painting by Mu-ch'i, 13th century.

Way people must follow had its starting point at the very creation of the universe, so no ideal could be older. Therefore, he himself had to be older in some sense than other significant thinkers of the time. He could not be as old as the roots of his philosophy, but the older the better.

His name, Lao Tzu, simply means Old Master, again to stress his seniority and the ancient origin of his thoughts. Lao Tzu was also the name mostly used in ancient China for the *Tao Te Ching*. It is still in wide use as the title for the book.

Whenever he actually lived his life, Lao Tzu's philosophy was regarded as one of the most ancient.

The legend about him says that he worked as a highly respected civil servant at the court of the emperor. At old age, he had grown tired of all the deceit, politics, and hypocrisy of the court, so he left the country riding on a water buffalo. This is the far most common depiction of him, heading for the border on a water buffalo.

At the western border, he stayed the night in the house of a border guard, who was so impressed by his wisdom that he urged Lao Tzu to write it down before leaving. So he did.

Then he crossed the border, and nothing more is known about his fate.

The Way and Virtue in 5000 Words

The result was a text of around five thousand words, divided into two parts. The first one started with the word *Tao*, the Way, and the second with the word *Te*, virtue. The word *Ching* refers to a book that has become a classic, a scripture revered as sacred, transmitting wisdom of old, fundamental to Chinese culture and philosophy.

The existing versions of the *Tao Te Ching* are still divided into two parts, and contain slightly more than five thousand words, the sum differing somewhat from one manuscript to the other. The presently known versions contain between 5,227 and 5,722 words.

The division into 81 chapters, though, is a later invention, probably made in the 1st century BC. The number of chapters is chosen to create the symmetry of 9 X 9, which has distinctive symbolic meaning in Chinese tradition. In the book, this division makes good sense in some cases and not at all in others.

In the original version, the text is not interrupted in any other way than occasional punctuation marks, which are not consequently used all through. Rhymes and other structures of the text suggest specific chapters – or verses, to be more accurate – as do the different subjects treated. Also, some such verses seem to be grouped according to subject, or related subjects. Still, none of this is done stringently enough to ascertain any division into chapters or verses of the whole book.

This structure, or lack thereof, has resulted in two main theories about the creation of the text. One is that its author simply wrote in a flowing manner, treating subjects as they occurred to him in the process, sort of like improvisation. The other theory is that the *Tao Te Ching* is a collection of traditional proverbs and other fragments of thought, without one single author.

Proverbs

The latter of those theories has been the most favored among Western experts. There are several reasons for it.

It's not uncommon among the classics that their author is not the one whose words are written down. It's true for the works of K'ung Tzu, Confucius, as well as for many other greats of human history, such as Socrates and Jesus. The words of most thinkers from ancient times have been preserved by other writers, sometimes much later than when they were supposed to have spoken them.

As for the *Tao Te Ching*, the text itself also seems to argue for being a compilation from different sources. The many short verses seem like proverbs, differing in style and content, and lacking in consistency. Usually, that's a sign of a work compiled from oral traditions.

Another argument for this is the fact that the whole text lacks specifics, by which to place it firmly in history. No emperors are mentioned, nor any historical events, not even any cultural characteristics that would date the work with some precision. It's unstuck in time. That, too, is often the case with oral traditions put into writing at a later time, especially in the case of proverbs, of course.

Most of the *Tao Te Ching* is written with rhymes, which is quite easy in the Chinese language. Rhyming is far from exclusive to oral tradition, but it's very common there. It made memorizing even long texts much easier. So, although it can't be used as evidence of an oral origin, it definitely suggests the possibility. Without rhymes, an oral origin would be much less likely.

Regarding the thoughts transmitted in the text, their ethereal nature and abstract cosmology suggest very old origins. This is far from certain, but philosophies of agrarian societies tend to advocate strict order of conduct, similar to books of law, and present a cosmology that is distinctly earthbound. This would apply to the thoughts of Confucius, but hardly to those of Lao Tzu.

Tao Te Ching presents a world order that has much more

in common with hunter-gatherer societies. Their cosmologies are usually very complex and abstract, not to say cryptic, and their ethics don't particularly stress hierarchy and obedience. I wouldn't say that Lao Tzu's Taoism is strictly pre-agrarian, but it gives an impression of such ideas clashing with the ideals of agrarian society. Taoism can be seen as an attempt of merging the two.

Now, if the verses in the *Tao Te Ching* precede the agrarian era, it's highly unlikely that they have one single author. They would be bits and pieces transmitted orally, from generation to generation, before the invention of writing made it possible to collect and preserve them.

On the other hand, there could very well be one person who did that job. That would make the legendary Lao Tzu the compiler of wisdom of old, where the proverbs gathered were those containing the same message – that of the Way and how it should be walked.

Actually, the text never claims anything else. It repeats frequently that it transmits the wisdom of old, and the sage it mentions so many times can also be a plural – all those wise ones in ancient times, who knew about the Way. Lao Tzu never claims to be the inventor of the ideas, but insists that he repeats what was well known by the ancestors. He states that he just compiles old material.

If Lao Tzu was the first to put the oral tradition into writing, it's still not sure if he did so with the *Tao Te Ching* in its entirety, as we know it today. He could have made a first version, which was then molded through other minds and added to by other contributors, before reaching its present state.

Frequent repetitions and other inconsistencies of the book suggest it. Some lines of the text are repeated, others appear with minor alterations, and some whole chapters seem to say the same as others, although with slightly different wordings.

One single writer would probably edit such things out, if not writing flowingly and ignoring an editing procedure. Especially a writer as scarce with words as the *Tao Te Ching* suggests, would avoid lengthy repetition.

So, if the *Tao Te Ching* is a collection of old proverbs, it was probably initially collected by one person, whom we can call Lao Tzu. But there would have been others contributing, before the text reached its present form. The extent of their contributions is difficult to ascertain. Probably, they mainly added other variations of the old proverbs, in an effort to make sure that nothing of this particular wisdom was lost.

They would have worked from a Taoist concept of sorts, not to deviate from the ideas and principles of the work. This suggests that the philosophy of Taoism was established in some form before this process.

It would be. Taoism contains ideas and perspectives that are very likely to have existed long before the beginning of agrarian society. Its philosophy of non-action, *wu-wei*, would make immediate sense in hunter-gatherer societies. Maybe it was sharpened and put into words in the clash with the emerging agrarian society, where so much in life suddenly became important and complicated.

Improvised Writing

The other basic theory about the birth of this text is that it was indeed written by one person, Lao Tzu, who did so out of his own mind and not by merely assembling old proverbs. If so, he was probably writing it in a flowing manner, somewhat like a musician improvises, not pausing much for editing or looking back at previous chunks of text.

This would actually fit quite well with the legend, which states that Lao Tzu wrote the *Tao Te Ching*, at the request of a border guard, the moment when he was about to leave China for good. Then he would not have bothered much with editing, nor would he have spent any significant amount of time on the text.

Five thousand words are not written in mere hours, so Lao Tzu would in this case surely have stayed as the guard's guest for at least a few days. That's not at all improbable. The guard was obviously delighted with his company. Considering his isolated job, he might have cheered at just about any visit.

The theory of one original author is also supported by the stringency of thought in the text and the consistent style in which it is written. *Tao Te Ching* is so sparse with words, and free of elaborate explanations, that it is partly almost cryptic. This seems more in line with the approach of one mind than the result of proverbs collected from all around.

The numerous examples of playing with words in similar manners suggest a certain kind of humor, which is also unlikely to be found in a mere collection of proverbs. So, the style and the consistency of thought are indications of a single mind behind the text.

Another thing that needs to be considered is the originality of the thoughts and ideas of the text. If it's a collection of old proverbs, it's unlikely to stand out from the mindset of the time. I can't say that I have the competence to consider this aspect with any confidence. It's not easy to ascertain what perspectives people were familiar with, some 2,500 years ago. But there are things that stand out.

Lao Tzu on a Chinese stone rubbing from the 13th century.

道德經

Although Tao was a well-known concept in China at Lao Tzu's time, it rarely stood on its own. There was Heaven's Way, an expression he also uses, and the Way of this and that, but a Way preceding every other way, even the world as well as its possible creator – that must have stood out.

Also, the sharp criticism of authorities, all the way up to the ruler of the country, was not likely to be repeated by many, at least not in writing.

The disrespect, with which Lao Tzu spoke about authorities, could be an explanation to the many missing chapters of the *Tao Te Ching* manuscript found in Guodian. Those that speak the most frankly about inadequate leadership are absent. The manuscript belonged to the tutor of a prince. He surely had to treat the subject delicately. Also chapters that praise the female over the male are missing.

In the firm hierarchy of ancient China, Lao Tzu's text was provocative, indeed.

The principle of non-action, *wu-wei*, might also have seemed somewhat out of place in the blooming empire of China, moving boldly towards increased splendor. Such a magnificent country would cherish something less humble.

Nor is Lao Tzu's praise of the female and the yielding very typical for any time or place. Actually, there's nothing excluding the possibility that Lao Tzu was a woman. That would explain the text's perspective from below and persistent sympathy for the people at the bottom of the ladder. Such emphasized empathy is not that common among male philosophers.

Well, none of these speculations have the weight of evidence, but at least they support the possibility that the *Tao Te Ching* was the work of one person's mind. The text certainly gives that impression and has been regarded as such, through most of history since its emergence. Its many readers through time have felt what has also been my impression: These words have the air of stemming from one brilliant mind.

Still, the book might have gone through significant changes, until it reached the form that we are familiar with. Some of them we know, such as the division into 81 chapters, which may very well have included other alterations in this process. There have also been some changes of the wording, here and there, that altered the meaning of these lines – or just clouded it.

This we know from recent discoveries of manuscripts that significantly predate the versions we until then had at our disposal.

Recent Findings

The findings in Mawangdui and Guodian, in the late 20th century, have clarified a lot about the *Tao Te Ching*. What had been pure speculation and guesswork was with those findings brought to conclusion. Some of these conclusions were expected, but there were also several that took the experts by surprise.

The biggest surprise was that these findings showed that the text had mainly been the same since much older times than previously assumed.

Until 1973, the manuscripts in existence didn't date farther back than to the 3rd century CE. They were commented copies, written by dignified Chinese scholars. The most famous and widely used one was that of the young genius Wang Pi, who lived in the 3rd century CE. It was the one used in almost all English translations.

But in 1973, two manuscripts of the *Tao Te Ching* were found in a Mawangdui tomb dating to 168 BC. These versions were written around 200 BC, one slightly older than the other. Both are practically complete, lacking only minor parts where the silk they were written on had been damaged.

Oddly, they reverse the order of the two parts of the text, putting *Te*, chapters 38-81, before *Tao*, chapters 1-37. A few of the chapters within these parts are also placed differently from the traditional order. Apart from these anomalies, the Mawangdui manuscripts showed a text that was surprisingly similar to the previously known versions.

So, here were two manuscripts, more than five hundred years older than the ones previously in our possession, and the deviations were quite minor. Obviously, this text had been preserved with great care and accuracy through the centuries. Also, it was clear that it had found its present form no later than at the start of the 2nd century BC. Many experts had previously guessed that it was a compilation done during that century or the next one.

After this finding, several experts revised their assumptions, saying that the text had probably found its present form in the 3rd century BC, most likely by the end of it. Those experts were soon to be proven wrong, yet again.

In 1993, a manuscript dating back another hundred years was found in a tomb in Guodian. It was written on bamboo straps, the method of the time. This manuscript, which is far from complete, is dated to around 300 BC, and the chapters it does contain are almost identical with later versions.

Now, many experts claim that the text was compiled somewhere during the 4th century BC, but I would hesitate

Silk sheets of the Mawangdui Tao Te Ching manuscripts from around 200 BC, discovered in 1973.

to make such a statement. Maybe it's time to accept the legend, making Lao Tzu a senior contemporary of K'ung Tzu, which would put him in the 6th century BC. That's where Chinese scholars prefer to place him.

The consistent form and content of the *Tao Te Ching*, already at 300 BC, strongly suggests that it was an established classic way before that time. Future archeological excavations will probably bring us older versions than the one in Guodian. There are lots of those going on in China.

There would not have been a lack of old manuscripts to begin with, if China had not been struck by systematic book burnings, now and then through its history. The first major one started already in 213 BC. There have been some Chinese emperors seeming to take Lao Tzu's warnings about knowledge literally, by trying to do away with literature.

Simple like uncarved wood
What the three newly found manuscripts have revealed is not just that the *Tao Te Ching* had been kept mainly intact through all this time, but also that the text is indeed written in a style signified by utter directness and clarity. Its topic might be clouded, but its words are, as Lao Tzu says in the 70th chapter, "very easy to understand."

Several strange lines, difficult to interpret, have been clarified by the three older manuscripts. Their language is as straightforward as their messages. Lao Tzu spoke without poetic decoration or rhetorical roundabouts. Not that it makes all of his cosmology and ethics clear as day, but he had no intention of complicating matters. To him, what he spoke about was probably self-evident.

Tao is the primordial natural law that the universe conforms to, since its emergence out of chaos. Because this is how things in the world are and should be, we need to do very little to adjust, other than look for its patterns in the small and seemingly insignificant details of existence. That's where Tao is hiding.

If we try to improve the world, especially if we do so without understanding Tao, we are sure to damage it. So, we should practice non-action, *wu-wei*, and enjoy the voyage that the Way offers. The less we aspire to accomplish, the less our disappointment will be. True satisfaction is to be found in accepting life as it is, instead of struggling to change it into something we imagine that we wish.

It's probably truer now, than ever before in human history. What we want is not what we need. What we long for makes us blind to what we have. What we are is not what we pretend to be. Only what we cease to cover up, we can see as it really is. Lao Tzu tells us that there's nothing we have to do to understand him. We will find the Way if we stop searching for it. It's right here.

Reaching the West

The first translation to a European language of the *Tao Te Ching* was done by the French priest Francois Noël (1651-1729), who had spent several years in China. He wrote it in Latin, which was the common thing to do at the time. This would have been in the beginning of the 18th century.

His translation passed almost unnoticed. Another Latin translation emerged in 1788, as a gift from India to the Royal Society of England. Its fate was similar to that of Noël's version. None of them was printed, so there were not many readers they could have reached.

The first printed translation was released in 1842. The French sinologist Stanislas Julien made it. After another thirty years, the first printed English versions came, and in 1891 James Legge's translation was published. Both his and Julien's versions are still in print.

During the end of the 19th century, there was a growing Western fascination with Eastern thought and culture, so the number of *Tao Te Ching* translations grew rapidly. Early in the 20th century, there were versions in just about every language. Even the English occultist Aleister Crowley made one, in his own incomparable way.

Today, the versions of Lao Tzu's text are almost countless. In English alone, there are probably more than a hundred. Some are made by accomplished sinologists, others by academics of more or less relevant disciplines. There are also versions made by poets, mystics, priests of different confessions, and so on. For example, the American novelist Ursula K. Le Guin, famous for her fantasy and science fiction stories, published an elegant version in 1997, which she made in collaboration with J. P. Seaton, a professor of Chinese.

Tao Te Ching has also been popularized by numerous books applying its philosophy more freely to present circumstances. Benjamin Hoff explored the Taoism he found in A. A. Milne's *Winnie the Pooh*. His first book on the subject, *The Tao of Pooh*, was published in 1982 and quickly became a bestseller all over the world. In 1993 he followed up with the unavoidable *The Te of Piglet*.

A few years ahead of Hoff, the physicist Fritjof Capra wrote a book where he daringly compared the outskirts of physics with the cosmological principles of Taoism and other ancient traditions. *The Tao of Physics* was published in 1975. In spite of its advanced subject, the book was a huge bestseller.

It also inspired a stream of books popularizing natural science by comparing it to ancient myths and beliefs. Gary Zukav's *The Dancing Wu Li Masters* from 1979 had a success similar to that of Capra's book.

Another bestseller writer in the field is Paul Davies, with a number of books comparing religious beliefs to modern physics, such as *God and the New Physics* from 1983 and *The Mind of God* from 1992. There are so many books dealing with this perspective, and so many writers behind them, that it could be called a literary genre.

Not all of them focus on Taoist principles, but the subtle cosmology of the *Tao Te Ching* makes it frequently referred to in such works.

Lao Tzu's universe, governed by a sublime natural principle instead of any gods, is attractive to speculating scientific minds of today. The ease by which his ideas can be applied to modern science makes his text more relevant than he would ever have guessed if he had a glimpse of our society, which must be as far from his modest ideal as ever possible.

But opposites attract. Maybe our increased interest in Lao Tzu's words stems from the urgent fact that we have reached a point where we really need to listen to them. Taoism may have been an oddity in ancient China, but in our world it has become a necessity.

Words as pictures

Chinese writing is done by pictograms, simplified pictorial representations of the words. Actually, a more proper word for it, when used as a written language, is logogram, as opposed to our Western phonogram that marks pronunciation. It's a fascinating world of symbols, filled with meaning and double-meaning. As the saying goes: A picture is worth a thousand words.

According to legend, this system of writing was invented already in the 27th century BC by Ts'ang-chieh, who served under the Yellow Emperor. Before that, the Chinese tied knots on ropes as a way of keeping certain records. This is mentioned in Lao Tzu's 80th chapter.

The oldest documented Chinese writing is from the late Shang Dynasty, around the 12th century BC, in the form of oracle bones. The Chinese logograms combine different uses

Turtle shell oracle bone from the late Shang Dynasty, around the 12th century BC.

of the simplified images they combine. There are basic signs, called radicals, like that of the mouth, an eye, the sun, a tree, and so on. Often in a word, they are combined with other signs specifying the word's meaning with varied degrees of abstraction, or with signs hinting at its pronunciation. The results are very complex and suggestive.

For example, the word *Tao* combines the signs for a step and a face, suggesting the notion of walking in the direction you are facing. Among the many speculations on the etymology of this logogram, is the drastic idea that it began as a depiction of the skulls of enemies put on poles on the way to towns, thereby warning visitors to beware.

The word *ch'i*, vital breath, combines the signs for rice and steam. Rice was and is the main food for the Chinese, but it needs to be boiled before consumption. *Te*, virtue, is quite complicated, containing the signs for walking, looking straight ahead, and the heart. We would call it walking the narrow road of righteousness.

In this book, there are several other examples of how Chinese words are combined, which is usually referred to as their etymology. They reveal a lot about the traditional Chinese mind and philosophy. Any learned Chinese will find great joy in contemplating their meaning.

This was certainly true also for Lao Tzu, when he used more than 5,000 words to write his book. For a proper and adequate understanding of it, at least in its vaguest expressions, one needs to take this into account. Lao Tzu was aware of the complexity of the signs he used, and played on it as he did on other aspects of the Chinese language.

Another thing that needs to be understood is how repetition gives different impressions in logograms compared to phonograms. Words written with pictures can be repeated frequently, without the same irritation of the reader as if it were done in a language of phonograms.

Lao Tzu's text is full of such repetition, starting from the very beginning, where there are three Tao among the first six words. In English, this is disturbingly repetitious, but with imagery it is instead rather intriguing, since it needs to be sort of deciphered.

It's a poetic riddle, comparable to Shakespeare's "To be or not to be." *Tao Te Ching* is full of it.

When translating the text, a proper balance is hard to find. If all those repetitions are included, there's a lesser poetic impression than the original text deserves, but editing them out would falsify the nature of the text.

In my translation, I have kept almost all of them. Instead I have used line breaks in an effort to recreate the simplicity with which one reads repetitions written by pictograms. That makes it easier for the eye to capture the pattern without having to drag through a lot of letters. It will also do as a kind of substitute for the fact that most of the *Tao Te Ching* is rhymed.

Spelling Chinese

The transcription of Chinese, how to write its words with Western letters, is not an exact science. Since Chinese texts are written with pictograms, little is stated about the actual pronunciation. That differs considerably through China, both geographically and historically. Without specifications of the sounds in their written language, this diversity was unavoidable.

There are two major methods of transcription at use today for Chinese words. *Pinyin* is the one presented by the modern state of China in the 1950's as the official system of transcription. Today, it's the system used almost exclusively, especially for anything contemporary.

In the case of the Chinese classics, though, an older system of transcription is well established and still in use. It's called *Wade-Giles* after its two creators, the latter of which published a Chinese-English dictionary based on it, in 1892. This system of transcription was the dominating one in the English language for most of the 20th century, so all the translated classics of that period used it. Therefore, it's the spelling we are still the most familiar with, especially in the case of the Chinese classics and their terminology.

The Chinese language is far from homogenous all over that great nation, and many of its pronunciations are quite alien to Western tongues. So, any transcription is bound to be imprecise. That goes for pinyin as well as Wade-Giles. No wonder, then, that there is an ongoing debate about what system to use for the Chinese classics, such as the *Tao Te Ching*.

Already for the word *Tao* (in pinyin *Dào*), much can be said against both transcriptions. The initial sound is somewhere between T and D, but still not pronounced in the way Western languages treats such sounds. Anyway, for most of the words, the two systems of transcription don't get that far apart. This can be seen in the examples below. If you are familiar with one spelling, you can often recognize the word also when spelled the other way.

In addition, Chinese is pronounced with a distinct melody, so that a word might rise in tone, lie flat, or fall. That's how the three words of *Tao Te Ching* are spoken: up at *Tao*, still at *Te*, and down at *Ching*, as if wording the shape of a hill. Not an easy language to transcribe.

For a while, pinyin seemed to take over in the new

translations and the literature on the subjects, but I have the impression that this development is halted. Wade-Giles is still in use and seems even to be preferred for the classics, at least outside purely academic writing.

In this book, I stick to Wade-Giles for all the words in Lao Tzu's text, as well as for names and terms related to it. If I'm not mistaken, only the names of the places where the oldest *Tao Te Ching* manuscripts were found, Guodian and Mawangdui, are spelled in the pinyin fashion. That's simply because the excavations were made recently, so I chose the established contemporary transcriptions.

Otherwise, I use Wade-Giles consistently. That way, too, it's much easier for the reader to compare this version to most of the previously existing ones in English.

Here are some examples of words and names, as they are transcribed according to Wade-Giles and pinyin:

Wade-Giles	*Pinyin*
Tao Te Ching	Dào Dé Jing (or Daodejing)
Lao Tzu	Lao Zi (or Laozi)
K'ung Tzu	Kong zi (or Kongzi)
Chuang Tzu	Zhuang Zi (or Zhuangzi)
I Ching	Yì Jing (or Yijing)
Ch'i	qì (or qi)
Yin yang	yin yáng (or yin yang)
T'ai chi	tàijí (or taiji)
Sheng jen	shèng rén
Wu-wei	wúwéi
Wang Pi	Wang Bi
Shih chi	Shiji
Ssu-ma Ch'ien	Sima Qian
Ma-wang-tui	Mawángdui (or Mawangdui)
Kuo-tien	Guodiàn (or Guodian)

Tao

The Way

道可道
非常道
名可名
非常名
無名天地之始
有名萬物之母
故常無欲以觀其妙
常有欲以觀其徼
此兩者同出而異名
同謂之玄
玄之又玄
眾妙之門

Chapter 1 of Tao Te Ching in Chinese. The Wang Pi version. On the previous page is a calligraphy of the sign for Tao, made by the author.

1

The Way that can be walked is not the eternal Way.
The name that can be named is not the eternal name.
The nameless is the beginning of Heaven and Earth.
The named is the mother of all things.

Therefore:
Free from desire you see the mystery.
Full of desire you see the manifestations.
These two have the same origin but differ in name.
That is the secret,
The secret of secrets,
The gate to all mysteries.

It's All Real

Lao Tzu begins his writing about *Tao*, the Way, by stating that the written word cannot fully encompass the real thing. The workings of the Way are hidden behind what we can observe. It was present at the dawn of time and the birth of the universe, but it's visible only through what has been created out of it, in accordance with it: the whole world and all its creatures. Tao is the Way the universe works.

But that also means it can be understood by observing what can be observed: the manifestations. When we indulge in the world as we perceive it, we might be blinded by the splendor and magnitude of it all, but we do witness the workings of the Way, which is the principle behind it. We don't see the interior, but the surface. Still, its shape reveals a lot about what it covers.

If we want to see beneath the surface, into what really makes up the world, we have to detach ourselves from the attraction of that surface. When we distance ourselves from the world as if we are not at all part of it, then we can see through it. The mystery of its true nature becomes evident.

This is like an echo of Buddhism, although preceding it. Truth is revealed to the one who detaches himself from the world, not tempted by anything in it and not distracted by any of its phenomena.

Because we allow ourselves to be consumed by the world, we can't see it clearly. If we cease to look at the world for what we hope or fear that it will be to us, then we can see what it really is – its true nature, which is the Way.

But we don't have to see through the world to manage living in it. The manifestation is an expression of the Way, so it's as real and essential as the Way itself. Like the two sides of a coin. The world can be understood from its surface as well as from its interior. The descriptive words will differ, but the world and its workings remain the same.

The surface is just as real as what lies beneath it. They reveal one another. None exists without the other, so none is superior or inferior.

Opposites

We tend to think in opposites – light or dark, high or low, hot or cold, and so on. That's fine as a method of getting acquainted with the world and beginning to understand how it works. But when we make judgments, calling one opposite good and the other bad, we are mistaken. They complement and depend on each other. Even when one of them seems obviously superior, neglecting the other is unwise.

道 *Tao (also spelled Dao), the Way. The pictogram consists of the signs for a head and a step – walking in the direction one faces. There are many theories about the original meaning of this sign.*

Many belief systems praise the spirit and condemn the body, but the latter is the vessel of the former. They depend on each other. A spirit without a body cannot act, nor can a body without spirit. The Taoist treats each according to its nature. Both of them need concern and nourishment. Whichever one is neglected, both will suffer.

The unity of surface and interior also tells us that we should not make them contradict. If you pretend to be something that you are not, then your outside and inside are in conflict. Somewhere along the way you will break. They don't need to be exactly the same. They cannot, since they differ in nature. But they are companions on one and the same path. A human being is a whole, walking one way. If this whole is divided, for whatever reason, you will halt. You get nowhere.

When we accept that the mystery and the manifestations mirror each other, the secret is revealed. We can understand all. What you see is what you get, but you have to truly see it for what it is.

The manifestations become clear when you observe them with delight. The mystery appears when you detach yourself from the world and empty your mind. You will discover their unity: something and nothing embrace, and become all.

道德經

2

When everyone in the world sees beauty,
Then ugly exists.
When everyone sees good,
Then bad exists.

Therefore:
What is and what is not create each other.
Difficult and easy complement each other.
Tall and short shape each other.
High and low rest on each other.
Voice and tone blend with each other.
First and last follow each other.

So, the sage acts by doing nothing,
Teaches without speaking,
Attends all things without making claim on them,
Works for them without making them dependent,
Demands no honor for his deed.
Because he demands no honor,
He will never be dishonored.

Don't Split the Unity

In the second chapter, Lao Tzu continues by presenting a consequence of what he stated in the first chapter. Because the opposites of existence are united in a necessary whole, it's detrimental to separate them – either in deed or in value.

The unity of opposites makes up the world. We should not call one good and the other bad. There is no point in telling them apart at all, since they cannot exist divided. Nor do they make any sense when separated from one another.

Certainly, we appreciate some things more than others, but we must remember that we are able to do so only because we can compare them. The ugly is the mirror of the beautiful. So, who can say that beauty is only within the latter? That's why we are unable to find complete consensus about which is which. What one of us regards as beautiful, another will watch with indifference.

It's even so that each of us changes the way we see things, from moment to moment and from one perspective to the other.

Beauty is no object in itself, but merely the impression of one. It's in the eye of the beholder, and not a fixed quality of that which is beheld. So, we should treat our preferences with the appropriate modesty. And we should learn to appreciate the beauty in the ugly, as well as the ugly in the beautiful. None exists without the other, but within each other.

Good and Bad

We hasten to call some things good and others bad, but fail to recognize that such opposites are also deeply dependent on one another. Judging between them has little meaning. The prickled stem leads up to the flower of the rose. A forest is rejuvenated by fire, as is the soil by the merciless turn of the seasons. Night brings repose from day, and death gives room for new life. One is in need of the other.

Even when it comes to human deeds, judging them as good or bad is a risky business for the most experienced judge, as well as for a jury of twelve. There is rarely just one person responsible for a series of events, and within that person there is sure to be a number of contradictions. So, trying to decide on the character of a person in terms of good and bad is even less likely to succeed.

We are more complex than any book can cover. No person is simply good or bad. Both extremes are inside of us, and in a multitude of nuances. Any personality is a mystery beyond explanation. We can only observe the actions by which that personality expresses itself.

What we do is the result of a series of events and reasons. Few of them are at our control. Most of our actions are not ones of choice, but of necessity. We stumble into them, or we are pushed. Certainly, we are still responsible for our deeds, but there is no point in judging them as good or bad. That only interferes with our ability to counteract them when needed, or support them when they are wanted.

Not to mention the problem of what is good for one but bad for another. That's mostly the case. Therefore, modern philosophers prefer to discuss ethics in quantities: what is good for most people, or what is more good for one than it is bad for another, and so on. There is rarely an objective truth to be found, or a value that everyone can share.

Mostly, good and bad are in the hands of those who have power. They decide what is good for all or bad for all. That's usually what happens to be good or bad for them. Lao Tzu has more to say about that attitude, later in the *Tao Te Ching*.

Deeds of people may force us to react, but we are not helped much by defining those deeds morally, or even deciding on moral standards for all.

We make rules to bring a working order to society and to push society in the direction we want it to develop. We follow these rules when we can, and break them when we cannot constrain ourselves. The rules stipulate what the consequences of breaking them should be. That's all fair and square. There is no need to add a moral judgment to the legal one. For that, we simply do not have enough information.

If we allow morals to influence our judgments, we are unable to be objective. Then there is a risk that the punishment of a deed is far worse than the deed itself.

So, the sage refrains from judging. He is very hesitant to interfere, or to insist that his opinion should be respected. He is reluctant to lead, and refuses to be followed. He is an example without pointing it out.

Since he never puts himself above others, they find no reason to rebuke him.

The Sage
Lao Tzu frequently mentions *sheng-jen*, which is translated 'the sage' in almost every English version of the *Tao Te Ching*. I spent quite some time pondering alternative translations, but found none better. It implies wisdom of a profound kind. Also, there's an archaic ring to it that fits well with the traditional Chinese idea about ancient times being superior, to which Lao Tzu evidently subscribed.

But the sage is not a person elevated above the rest of mankind. To Lao Tzu, anyone can be sage by simply following Tao. Those who do so excel mostly at being humble, not at all separating themselves from their fellow men. The sage is someone like you and me, but he or she has achieved true wisdom. *Sheng-jen* is a person with a refined spirit, who is modest about his place in the world and shows compassion towards others, whatever the level of their wisdom.

The word *sheng* is written with a sign that contains three

Sheng-jen, the sage.

parts: an ear, a mouth, and the sign for a king or sovereign. Someone who listens and speaks beyond the perspective of common men. A refined mind. It's closer to what we call reason than to knowledge. We are reminded of King Salomon of the Bible, who listened carefully to his subjects and then spoke wisely to them. He was a sensible ruler, who knew not to speak before listening. The king commanded according to what he found out from using his ears.

Lao Tzu has little respect for the ones who call themselves learned and clever. Instead, he stresses the superiority of simple reason, what we call common sense. To Lao Tzu, the sage is someone who excels at common sense.

We will learn more about what Lao Tzu regarded as true wisdom in the following. He used the expression *sheng-jen* more than thirty times in the *Tao Te Ching*.

The word *jen* simply means a human being, a person. It's often used like the word 'man' is in English. It may refer to a male person, but just as well to human beings of any gender. Lao Tzu certainly had no problem with the possibility of women being truly wise. On the contrary, as will be seen frequently in the following chapters, he tended to regard the female qualities as far superior to the male ones.

He might have expected more women than men to be sage. Actually, what's to say that Lao Tzu wasn't a woman?

The Chinese text rarely specifies gender, either regarding the sage or other characters referred to in the *Tao Te Ching*. In the English language this would get awkward, so I've had to give it up on several occasions. In such cases I have chosen the male gender, just because the tradition of its use in such a context makes it slightly more neutral than the use of the opposite gender would.

So, please regard any 'he' in the text as 'he or she.' That's true for my comments as well as for Lao Tzu's chapters.

3

Not praising the deserving
Prevents envy.
Not valuing wealth
Prevents theft.
Not displaying what's desirable
Prevents confusion of the senses.

Therefore:
The sage governs by emptying senses and filling bellies,
Curbing strife and strengthening backs,
Keeping the people ignorant and without desire,
Making the learned afraid to act.
If he acts without action, order will prevail.

As Little as Possible

Society is obsessed with the eagerness to change. Change for the better, we would like to believe. Today we call it progress, as if that's automatically the case. We encourage impatience and hurry onward, convinced that letting go of the past will bring an increasingly splendid future.

This mentality is doomed to escalate and accelerate, until we have no time at all to compare our innovations with what they replace. We don't know if they are improvements. We don't even know what they lead to at length.

One day, we might destroy our world without even realizing it.

Non-Action
Lao Tzu is wary of change, of interfering with the present state of things. He sees the world as one of precious balance, where action that is not carefully considered might easily lead to an avalanche of unwanted effects, before balance is restored. So he praises non-action, *wu-wei*. Do as little as possible, and only when you absolutely have to. Minimum interference ensures maximum stability.

The more power you have, the more important it is to stick to non-action. A good ruler has the patience to refrain from action before knowing exactly what to do, and then to do as little as possible. Even for great problems, small solutions are usually the safest – and the most efficient. Big solutions cause new problems of equal size.

There are those who claim to know what is needed, but they seldom know what needs may arise out of their solutions. So, they don't know enough. Knowledge is also power and should be treated with the same concern.

The ones who know the most should be the most humble about the certainty of their knowledge. If they are aware of the risk of being proven wrong by a future in the direction of their suggestion, they will be hesitant to propagate it. That's how they can make their responsibility equal to their knowledge.

Moderation
Mankind is a longing species. Each of us knows that we are mortal, so we are desperate to live our lives to the fullest. This makes us easy victims of greed and envy. We guard each other with envy, suffering to the extent that others seem to enjoy themselves, struggling for a surplus surpassed by none, losing any sense of what is enough.

Wu-wei, non-action.

Greed makes it impossible to delight in what we have, since there will always be more to get. This cannot last.

Lao Tzu's cure for such galloping madness is moderation in all. Only if we cease to crave for what we don't possess, we can appreciate what we have. If so, we will find that we don't need much at all. Anything beyond food to keep us from getting hungry is a luxury that we can do without. Any other power than the strength to endure is a burden.

We live in a society of mass consumption. All of us are both producers and consumers, but we tend to forebear the former just for the reason of being able to indulge in the latter. Should we not be happier about what we are able to create than what we hurry to waste? At least, we should be able to ask ourselves if we really want everything that we set our eyes on.

The joy of giving in to greed is quickly replaced by the disappointment of its minute reward. That's the trap of longing. Few things are as pleasing when we get them, as they were tempting when we longed for them.

We must learn the deep and lasting pleasure of discovering how much it is that we do not need. Thereby we also learn how much we already have, and how precious that is.

4

The Way is empty, yet inexhaustible,
Like an abyss!
It seems to be the origin of all things.
It dulls the sharpness,
Unties the knots,
Dims the light,
Becomes one with the dust.

Deeply hidden, as if it only might exist.
I do not know whose child it is.
It seems to precede the ancestor of all.

The Hidden Cause

Lao Tzu returns here to the mysterious nature of Tao, the Way. It's so vague and distant that we can only guess its existence by the deductions we make from observing the world around us. It's the inner working of the universe, and probably therefore also the originator of it.

Tao is the natural law by which the universe operates.

A natural law has no form of its own, but governs all there is, and never gets fatigued or diminished. Although it causes all the magnificence of the world we live in, it's infinitesimal, like the dust of the dust.

This law that governs all can have no preferences. It treats the biggest things the same as the smallest, none with less care. To Tao, they are essentially the same.

Mountains, planets, galaxies, they all consist of atoms, which do in turn consist of particles so minute that their

Ti, supreme god in Chinese mythology. The sign also means emperor.

existence may never be confirmed. Since everything in the world consists of things small, the minute is closer to the nature of Tao. And since most things in the world go by unnoticed, the hidden is also closer to the nature of Tao.

Because Lao Tzu sees the Way as the reason behind all, he concludes that it must have the most to do with the things that we regard as lesser. The big events are rare, while everyday proceedings take place constantly. The bigger the size of things, the fewer they are. So, the Way deals mainly with the small.

We should ponder this, so that we remember to pay the most attention to the things that seem to be the least significant.

The most enduring powers in the world are those that stand out the least. Sharpness does not last, nor does the tightness of a knot, or the brightest light. There is nothing that remains longer than its own dust.

So, if we become like dust, we will prevail – and we will be in unison with Tao.

That has not been the typical trait of mankind so far. Instead, we ravel at burning down forests to build temples and palaces, drilling tunnels through mountains, and changing the courses of rivers. Ours is noisy species.

A Vague Deity

The last line of this chapter is the only clear occurrence of a divine entity in the *Tao Te Ching*. What I have translated as the ancestor of all is *Ti*, who was the first and supreme god in ancient Chinese mythology.

Although Ti was indeed regarded as a creator god, Lao Tzu doubts that he predates Tao. Even a creator god must obey the natural laws that rule the universe, or it would not have come into existence. If it did, it would not have remained.

A natural law does not exist by itself, but through nature, where it manifests itself. Therefore, it has no birth date. There may be a starting point for its manifestation, but the law itself is timeless. When a world of whatever kind appears, it has to follow the law for such a world. But the law does not change if the world appears or disappears. It remains the same forever and anywhere. So, it's eternal and ever-present. It was before the gods, and it's present where they are not.

There can be a universe without any gods to rule it, but not one without laws for it.

Lao Tzu, the Old Master. Calligraphy by the author.

5

Heaven and Earth are not kind.
They regard all things as offerings.
The sage is not kind.
He regards people as offerings.

Is not the space between Heaven and Earth like a bellows?
It is empty, but lacks nothing.
The more it moves, the more comes out of it.

A multitude of words is tiresome,
Unlike remaining centered.

The Limit of Compassion

This chapter consists of three parts that have little to do with one another. The first part talks about offerings, the second about a bellows, and the third about words.

The division of the *Tao Te Ching* into 81 chapters was not done by its author, but introduced much later. So, here I suspect that three separate sayings have been combined into one, although Lao Tzu did not intend it.

The first part speaks of a ruthlessness that seems terrifying. The offerings that Lao Tzu mentions were straw dogs used in religious rituals, and discarded afterward. We have no doubt that nature treats all its components and creatures with such indifference, simply because it lacks awareness. Storms whip the forests, oceans chew on land, winter kills what summer nourished, and beast feeds on beast that feeds on beast. It's like a machine.

But why should the sage do the same? Should we not be compassionate and do our utmost to save fellow men from pain and misfortune?

Well, Lao Tzu probably refers to society as a whole – like nature is a whole. Too much concern for single individuals can bring mayhem on society. We should be like straw dogs in the sense that none is worth more than the survival of the society that contains us all.

So, the sage would not dream of harming society for the benefit of a few of its members. On the other hand, he would not hesitate to sacrifice a few for the need of all. To guarantee the survival of society, he would be prepared to offer almost all of its inhabitants.

Anyone who is given the power to rule a nation would do the same. Actually, people demand it of their ruler. It's the very basis of any society. Nothing within it is worth sacrificing all of society for, and no price is too high to save it from destruction.

This is not only the case in a crisis, but in everyday life as well. Individuals cannot demand to be treated better than what is good for the whole. On the other hand, there is no reason for making the citizens suffer more than what is needed for society to prevail.

The most precious society is the one that needs the least sacrifice of its members.

Procreation between Heaven and Earth

In the second part of this chapter, Lao Tzu marvels at the abundance of the world we live in – the space between Heaven above our heads and Earth below our feet.

In this space we move about freely, and there seems to be no end to what is brought forth in it: countless genera-

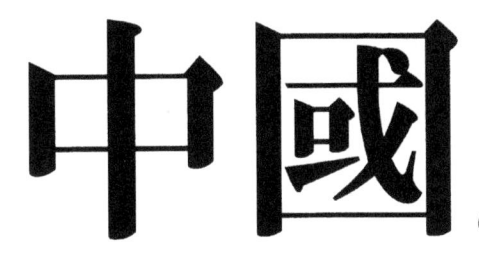

China, the Middle Kingdom.

tions of animals and vegetation, the cycles of the seasons, the splendor of sunrise and sunset, the phases of the moon. Everything moves and renews itself. The creatures feed on what grows from the earth, they breathe the sky, and they multiply.

The world is filled with tireless reproduction. It's as if the sky is a breath of life, its winds stirring the cornucopia that is Earth.

Truth in Silence
In the third part of the chapter, Lao Tzu seems aching to halt his writing, although he is only in the beginning of his book.

Words and the thoughts behind them may be clever, perhaps inspired, but still there can be enough of them. Then it's better to take it all in silently. We don't need to describe everything we experience, or to express all that we learn. Words are mere shadows. If we focus on them we may lose sight of the reality they try to imitate.

Instead, we should trust that our inner stillness finds the Way, and makes us see the patterns in the constant bombardment of information that is our daily life.

The word 'centered' in my translation of this chapter is *jhong* (or *zhong*) in Chinese. It means middle or center. It's used in the name for China (*Jhongguo* or *Zhongguo*, the Middle Kingdom), which makes the word a strong symbol indeed for its people. The Chinese pictogram for the word is a simplification of an arrow hitting the center of a target.

In Lao Tzu's use of the word, inner balance and steadfastness is implied, somewhat like the keel of a boat that's unaffected by the waves on the sea. That's how the human mind should be – calm in whatever turmoil surrounds it, confident even in a rain of urgent questions.

The answers are to be found in that calm.

6

The valley spirit never dies.
It is called the mystical female.
The entrance to the mystical female
Is called the root of Heaven and Earth.

Though gossamer,
As if barely existing,
It is used but never spent.

The Womb

Lao Tzu allows himself some play with words here. The Chinese word for valley, *ku*, can be translated gorge, and the word for female (of any species) also refers to a deep gorge. The word for mystical, *hsüan*, can be translated dark or deep. So, Lao Tzu describes a dark depth, from the entrance of which the whole world springs, like a child does from its mother's womb.

    The sign for entrance, also meaning gate or door, shows a swinging door, just like the one to the saloon in every Western movie. In the context of this chapter, it's an image also suggesting the gate to a woman's womb, which is certainly a birthplace of tremendous significance.

    To Lao Tzu, the origin of the world is female, like a mother of any species. Heaven and Earth are rooted at the entrance to this womb, but there is a vast depth beneath the entrance, from which so much more can emerge. This mother of all is endlessly fertile. She never ceases to breed and nurture.

道德經

Ku, the valley (left) and men, gate (right).

This mystical female is Tao, the Way. Again an intriguing imagery. The way to this primordial female leads into the dark gorge.

Tao as a mother of all, like the Greek Earth goddess Gaia, is a returning theme in the *Tao Te Ching*. Although ancient China was indeed a patriarchal society, Lao Tzu praised the traditionally female qualities repeatedly. Since the nature of Tao resembles the female much more than the male, so should people behave. Giving instead of taking, humble instead of proud, yielding instead of forcing, and so on.

This preference must have been very radical in the days of Lao Tzu. Actually, it still is.

In the last line of this chapter, Lao Tzu leaves the metaphor of the womb, although he still talks about Tao. He moves on to another aspect of it, another way of looking at it. The essence of the Way is as vague and fine as cobweb, because it's a principle, a natural law, with no substance of its own. That's why it lasts, no matter how much it is used. Like a formula.

7

Heaven is eternal and Earth is lasting.
How can they be eternal and lasting?
Because they do not live for themselves.
That is how they can be eternal.

Therefore:
The sage puts himself last and becomes the first,
Neglects himself and is preserved.
Is it not because he is unselfish that he fulfills himself?

Unselfishness

The well-known reward for the unselfish is the praise received. Another benefit is hinted in the example of Heaven and Earth: The ones who don't live for themselves will endure, because that path is less straining, less of a struggle.

Those who strive to get ahead are quickly fatigued and wear themselves down. Impatience and discontent are poison to the mind, therefore to the body as well. That's how it works. The one who chases his own happiness will never catch it. He just rushes from the cradle to the grave. He may reach far and gather a fortune, but when will he have time to enjoy it?

The humble ones with modest demands are easily satisfied and therefore soon to be joyous. Their joy lasts, because it's undisturbed by temptation. Such an attitude towards life is appeasing to the mind and a remedy for the body.

There is no guarantee for longevity, but those who are

pleased with their situation have a better chance at it than those who never get enough.

Of course, the reward for unselfishness can create a paradox. Considering such a reward, what selfish man would not try his utmost to be unselfish – at least enough to receive the benefits of it? That would be selfish unselfishness.

I doubt that it matters, though. We shape our lives and affect the lives of others by our deeds, not by the thoughts behind them. A good deed is helpful, whatever the reason for it. Considering the sad state much of the world is in, we can't afford to be picky. A good deed does good, even if its purpose is selfish.

Furthermore, it's quite possible that a selfish benefactor will be so pleased with the outcome that he forgets his original intention. That's one of the finer sides of mankind – delight and pleasure are contagious. Unfortunately, so are bitterness and anger. Another reason for encouraging good deeds of whatever intent.

8

Supreme good is like water.
Water greatly benefits all things, without conflict.
It flows through places that people loathe.
Thereby it is close to the Way.

A good dwelling is on the ground.
A good mind is deep.
A good gift is kind.
A good word is sincere.
A good ruler is just.
A good worker is able.
A good deed is timely.

Where there is no conflict, there is no fault.

Good

Clearly, this chapter continues the reasoning of the previous one, concerning the nature of good deeds. The unselfish one makes good deeds out of reflex, without thinking. That's automatic, when following the Way. For the rest of us, it's more complicated.

But we don't need to concern ourselves with the intricate fabric of ethics, when we try to make good deeds. What is far more important is that we discover what action is really for the better, and what might be for the worse. We need to understand the mechanics between action and consequence, in order to choose the former wisely.

Lao Tzu uses the example of water, one of the basic elements of nature, existing in tremendous abundance. Because it's such an important part of nature, it cannot do wrong. It shows what is natural. So we should follow its example.

The essence of water is its yielding. It flows downwards, as if constantly aspiring to be the lowest of all, and it does so with a minimum of force, rounding obstacles instead of striking at them, caressing its surroundings instead of tearing at them. Water willingly floats downwards, and there is no place too low for it. Still, it's essential to all living things.

Although we all drink from it, the water of the world is continuously replenished, from above and from below. Without it, we would perish. Indeed, for something of this magnificent importance, it's right to be modest and yielding, not to provoke all of those who are dependent on it.

The Primordial Sea

Lao Tzu's choice of water as an example to us all makes additional sense, when we consider the significance of water in ancient myths and beliefs.

In most cosmologies of old, the sea was regarded as the original and eternal element of the world. The primordial sea occurs in many creation myths, and the act of creation is often one of emergence from that sea. The Earth and all its creatures are born out of the sea. This is true for the biblical creation in the first book of Genesis, as well as in many other myths around the world.

When Lao Tzu describes Tao, the Way, as something akin to water, this might be based on creation myths old already at his time, where the world was believed to have emerged from a primordial sea. If so, it could almost be said that Tao actually is that primordial water, at least in essence. The Way is the principle of water, the mother of all.

Indeed, present science agrees that the ancestors of all the living creatures on Earth emerged from the sea. That was the initial womb of life on Earth. So, we cannot go wrong if we make it our teacher of how to live our lives.

Complicated Matters Made Easy
Now, Lao Tzu uses the example of water, when listing what is to recommend for man in several important aspects of our lives. These recommendations are straightforward enough, mostly self-evident. But we should not be fooled by the simplicity of these advices. They are profound, and not that easy to follow.

To make our dwellings on the ground is making sure that they will stand, so that we can trust them to protect us. To keep our minds deep is to respect that there is no such thing as a simple problem and a quick solution to it.

About gifts, we must understand that no matter how grand they are, they need to be beneficial to the receiver of them, and they should be given without ulterior motive, only out of kindness. Otherwise they are not gifts, even if that's what we call them.

When we speak to each other, we need to have an honest intent – even if circumstances force us to lie. Especially, we should not misuse our praise. We must always mean it, or we rob ourselves of words to use when that's indeed the case. It may be polite of us to greet everyone we meet with a compliment, but this is just decoration that must be used with care, or we are blinded by it. There are so many moments in life when words are precious, so that's how they should always be treated.

Any ruler needs to be just, no matter how difficult that may be at times. Any ruler. That includes a parent settling an argument between the children, as well as an emperor deciding the fate of his captured enemy. Ruling is an act of responsibility, never to be taken lightly.

Sometimes very grave decisions have to be made, maybe so much so that no compassionate man or woman can bear to make them. But there is no blame if the decisions are just. Then, the unfortunate ones who had to make them will be able to live with the memory.

On the other hand, if such a decision is unjust, it will forever gnaw on the one who made it. No matter if we call it conscience or something else, this gnawing is a malady with little hope of a cure. The unjust ruler may survive such decisions, maybe even seemingly profit tremendously from them, but at length the gnawing will take its toll. It can easily plague a whole life, all the way to the very bitter end.

A worker who is not competent at his craft, whatever it is, will not be very pleased with the result, nor will he enjoy all those daily hours spent on it. We need to cultivate our abilities and try to excel at our work, or there is no satisfaction. Since we all spend most of our days at work, it's very important to us that we feel fulfilled by it.

Sadly, there are so many professions nowadays, where people are regarded as little more than machines, expected to produce the simplest things in high quantities, as if that's all they can. Lao Tzu would not approve. We need to be able, and to feel able, which means that we must be allowed the chance to explore our abilities properly. Otherwise we cannot take pride in what we do, and we fail at being pleased with how we participate in society.

If there is one thing of primary importance with a good deed, it has to be its timeliness. Neither too early nor too late will do. But timeliness also means that we are alert to the needs of others, so that we can help them when the time comes. To be timely is to always be compassionate. It does not at all mean that we should postpone a good deed until we are certain that the time is good for it. We should always be eager to help each other. Then we will do so just in time, without thought.

If we practice such a compassionate alertness instead of constantly watching the clock, it will be fine. That's true also for other considerations. The important good deeds usually need little planning, but they need to be done even when there are obstacles. That's timeliness, as well. It's done when it needs to be done, no matter what.

Win-Win

The final line of this chapter returns to the principle of the water and its yielding nature. It finds its way through any terrain. This is possible also for our actions. There is always a way to act that doesn't collide with the intentions of others. If there is not, then we have already traveled far too long down the wrong path.

The ideal for any solution should be that everyone involved is pleased with it. Otherwise, it's probably not the final solution. In the world of business, this is called a win-win situation. Any business deal should be such, or the price of it will rise for all those involved, in one way or other.

The essence of a conflict is that some want to get what others don't want to give up. This really means that we focus on the other one's loss, rather than on our own gain. If we concentrate on the gain, we are sure to find a solution where it is shared. If we don't have that goal, we are just as sure to share the loss.

道德經

Therefore, the very best way to find a solution is not to search for one's own gain, but for that of the others involved. If you begin by understanding and respecting that, you will be surprised by how easy it is to reach an outcome beneficial to you, as well. If all people do the same, the world will shine.

9

*Filling all the way to the brim
Is not as good as halting in time.
Pounding an edge to sharpness
Will not make it last.
Keeping plenty of gold and jade in the palace
Makes no one able to defend it.
Displaying riches and titles with pride
Brings about one's downfall.*

To retreat after a work well done is Heaven's Way.

Moderation in All

Lao Tzu ends this chapter with the expression Heaven's Way, *T'ien chih Tao*, instead of just Tao, the Way. Still, the two expressions are definitely meant to be synonymous. I discuss this more in chapter 73, where Heaven's Way also appears.

The modesty and moderation suggested in this chapter are at the core of Lao Tzu's teaching. This he concludes from observing the discreet and yet omnipotent workings of Tao, the Way, as the ruling law of nature. Mankind should behave in the same manner. That means moderation in all.

The life he recommends is hardly spectacular, at least not on the surface. Any excess is sure to cause trouble. People should live their lives humbly, sort of discreetly. This goes for kings, too. Don't rock the boat.

The reward lies in peace and harmony of the mind, and a life lived with ease.

天之道

T'ien chih Tao, Heaven's Way.

Lao Tzu finds concrete examples showing the necessity of his ideal. If you fill the cup to the brim, you just risk spilling. It's a waste. In the Bible, this is called gluttony. Sometimes we are like children, biting off more than we can chew. It will not only wear us down, but it will also make everything taste more bland than it would if we consumed it with some restrain.

If you hammer a blade it may get sharp, but also fragile. It breaks easily, and then what good is its sharpness? In life, this is pushing things. It happens easily when we try to make something more out of what we have at our disposal. Whether this is driving a car faster than it's manufactured to manage, or forcing our own bodies and minds to feats beyond their capacity, the outcome is likely to be very unfortunate.

Money Costs

If you assemble riches, you will certainly attract people who want to take them away from you. Either they succeed, and you have nothing, or you spend your life struggling to protect your fortune. Then you have little time to enjoy it. That's just as true today as it was thousands of years ago. If anything, holding on to one's wealth has become increasingly complicated.

Present day society is obsessed with money, and it's taken for granted that being rich guarantees happiness. We assume that it must be fortunate to have a big fortune. But upon scrutiny we rarely find this to be the case. Instead, life becomes a kind of imprisonment, slavery under the obsession. The more money you have, the more it dominates your life.

A poor man's dream about getting rich is much more pleasant than a rich man's fear of becoming poor. Money is seductive, but a steep price must be paid for it. Actually, it costs you the joy that money was supposed to bring.

Fame Brings Envy

Titles and elevated positions in society are just as deceptive as money. They cause envy and animosity. Others want to bring you down, either to replace you or just so they don't have to look up to you.

Lately, fame has become the great quest. People think that if they just get famous, their lives will be splendid like the lives of celebrities, as seen in magazines and on TV shows. But that's just entertainment. It's a gilded version of reality. Under its shiny surface there is not much that separates the celebrities from the rest of us – except the fear of losing their fame.

Yes, fame is like money: It's much more of a torment to fear losing it, than it is to dream about reaching it.

Undisclosed Benevolence

In the last sentence, Lao Tzu states what is repeated many times in the *Tao Te Ching*: Do good without demanding praise for it. Then you act according to the highest ideals. So does Tao in ruling the world discretely by its laws. Nature obeys without being aware of any rules for its behavior. The mightiest force is the least visible.

This discretion of the laws of the universe is evident in the perspective of quantum physics, where the very smallest components are said to contain the rules by which all the stars and galaxies of the cosmos abide. There is no struggle involved in it. The world behaves according to its attributes, which are carried by particles too small to be seen in any microscope.

So, every human being should work with the same modesty. Also, when you don't demand any praise for your deeds, there is no reason for others to question them.

10

Can you make your soul embrace the One
And not lose it?
Can you gather your vital breath
And yet be tender like a newborn baby?
Can you clean your inner reflection
And keep it spotless?
Can you care for the people and rule the country
And not be cunning?
Can you open and close the gate of Heaven
And act like a woman?
Can you comprehend everything in the four directions
And still do nothing?

To give birth to them and nourish them,
Carry them without taking possession of them,
Care for them without subduing them,
Raise them without steering them.
That is the greatest virtue.

Modest Omnipotence

There is great power in attaining the wisdom Lao Tzu describes in his book, but anyone reaching that wisdom first and foremost learns the importance of modesty. This is a contradiction, almost a paradox.

It can be compared to what Jesus said about the meek: They are blessed, for they shall inherit the earth (Matthew 5:5).

Not that modesty is the moral obligation of somebody

enlightened and elevated. Lao Tzu makes few arguments of that kind in the *Tao Te Ching*. Instead, modesty is the conclusion, the key to how the world works according to Tao. Without modesty, neither Tao nor the world can be properly understood.

"The One" in the first line of this chapter is no doubt Tao, the Way. If your soul grasps it, how can you keep your soul from escaping you? How can you remain sound and in control of your senses?

Modesty is the solution. You observe the inner workings of the universe, but you understand that there is little to do about it. Nothing has changed as a result of your understanding. So you remain grounded in yourself, although you have grasped the secret of the universe.

The secret lies in the calm primordial law that arranged all according to the principle of effortlessness. The greater the power, the less its effort is. So, modesty surpasses pride and keeps you sane in the middle of the cosmic spectacle.

It's the same with the power so grand that it allows you to open and close the very gates of heaven, as if you were a god. Still, you should have no ambition, but be caring like a mother and accept the yielding position which was traditionally that of the woman.

You should have no wish to rule, or to make use of the powers you have at hand. Then you understand when to do nothing, which is usually the best.

To Lao Tzu, this attitude is the female one, and he definitely prefers it – for men as well. Traditionally, men have sought power and were eager to use it in abundance, while women preferred to leave things be, in order to do the least damage. That's the wisdom of doing nothing.

氣 *Ch'i, the vital breath.*

The Vital Breath

The vital breath that Lao Tzu mentions is *ch'i* (also transcribed *qi*). He uses the term in chapter 42 and 55, too. This is a fundamental concept in the cosmology of ancient China. It's a life energy filling the cosmos as well as mankind, an essence without which there is no life. It flows through us and around us, similar but not identical to the air we breathe. It's what is treated in acupuncture, by stimulating its meridians inside the body. It's also essential in the practice of *qigong*, the martial arts, and many other traditions.

The idea of such a life force is present in many other cultures. In India it's called *prana*, in old Greece *pneuma*, in Israel and the Arab world *ruach*. The Latin word is *spiritus*, the spirit, as in the biblical concept of the Holy Spirit.

The Chinese concept is mainly, at least in Lao Tzu's perspective, a nourishing power at man's disposal, of which we can have more or less, according to how we exercise it. Its nourishing quality is evident in the components of its pictogram.

Ch'i consists of two parts. One is the sign for rice, and the other that for steam or air. This suggests boiling rice, the way to make the basic food of the East edible. Indeed, the boiled rice is what has kept the Chinese alive for thousands of years. So, the sign suggests essential nourishment without which one cannot live.

Lao Tzu seems to have had an uncomplicated and straightforward view on ch'i as a vital essence in man, stronger in some than in others. What he asks in the tenth chapter is whether you are able to remain soft and gentle, even if this spirit of yours is strong.

Power tempts us to express it, and this ambition hardens us. When we are eager to show our strength, our muscles stiffen and our movements get clumsy. Our behavior becomes rude, and we easily damage our surroundings as well as ourselves.

The flow of ch'i through one's body may be weak like rain or strong like a waterfall, but our attitude should remain the same. Strength is no reason to use force.

Virtuous Caring
The last few lines of the chapter speak about "them," meaning people, from the perspective of a parent, a leader, an elder, or a ruler. It's all the same. Whatever your role, you must treat people as gently as if you had no power at all over them. Even if you are in the position to give orders, you should ask. Even though you are sure that you know what's right for them, you must allow them to choose for themselves.

You can suggest and assist, but not command. That will only lead to opposition and conflict. Also, it robs people of the chance to come to their own sound conclusions. You should treat people around you like loving parents treat their children.

Parents, too, must understand not to use force on the children in their care. Gentle guidance should be enough, preferably so that they are unaware of being guided. Children as well as adults need to feel that they have their future in their own hands. Only then are they able to listen to advice wholeheartedly, and follow them without frustration or remorse.

The greatest virtue of such a respectful attitude is its gentleness, its refusal to use the power at hand. This is in accordance with Tao, the Way, which acts in the same discreet manner. No virtue is greater than to be like Tao.

In chapter 51, Lao Tzu describes this very gentleness of Tao, ending it with the exact same phrase about the greatest virtue. Of course, Tao is nothing but the greatest virtue.

The Chinese word translated to virtue is *te*, which is also in the title of the book. I will return to it in coming chapters.

11

Thirty spokes are joined in the wheel's hub.
The hole in the middle makes it useful.
Mold clay into a bowl.
The empty space makes it useful.
Cut out doors and windows for the house.
The holes make it useful.

Therefore, the value comes from what is there,
But the use comes from what is not there.

The Necessity of Emptiness

This chapter, with its focus on the essential role of emptiness, could just as well be a Zen saying. Surely, Lao Tzu made this observation with a smile on his face. The paradox of emptiness making so many things useful is amusing.

In Zen, emptiness is taken much more seriously. If there is a purpose to be pointed out in Zen meditation, it's to strip oneself of any unnecessary thought to reach the state of an empty mind. This mental emptiness is regarded as the foremost clarity, a wisdom liberated from knowledge. It's not far from the ideal of the *Tao Te Ching*.

Lao Tzu returns to the subject from several different angles. He propagates the superiority of doing nothing, of keeping people ignorant, of presupposing nothing, and so on. This brings his ideas close to those of Zen. But he has other reasons. To him, this is the conclusion one reaches from studying the order and workings of the universe.

Emptiness is not something by which the human mind

advances, but finds its roots. When we realize the significance of emptiness in nature, we return to it and become again in harmony with it. Because nature operates by emptiness, so should mankind.

When Lao Tzu states that the value comes from what is there, but the use from what is not, he strongly advocates the latter. The value of what is visible and palpable is an illusion. It has no use without that which is absent. What is of no use has no value.

Bringing Order to Chaos

The use, the function, is closer to Tao, because Tao is present through how it works and how it makes the world work. One could say that it's much more a verb than a substantive. Therefore, an object without a function is as meaningless as the chaos that existed prior to the order introduced to the universe by Tao.

Although Lao Tzu seems to have cared very little for decorations, his statement does not exclude them completely from what can be valued in this world. Beauty is a function, and indeed there is a lot of necessary emptiness in the arts. Music is played on the silence between the tones, as well as on the tones. Great novels intrigue us with what is not spelled out. Paintings fascinate us by what they omit. Dance enchants by moments of stillness.

Nothingness is present everywhere. Without it, chaos would return. So, in the universe of the *Tao Te Ching*, order was accomplished by introducing emptiness into the full, balancing something with nothing. Emptiness is a blessing, without which it would all be too much.

We need to remind ourselves of this simple fact. Music soothes the soul, but not if we listen to it constantly. Colors delight our eyes, but more so when they are handled with some restrain. Dance invigorates, but excess fatigues us. Everything should be enjoyed moderately, and we should make sure to have generous portions of tranquil emptiness in our lives.

Maybe the best symbol of this is a work of calligraphy, where the black ink forms an intriguing character – but only because so much of the paper is left white, untouched by the brush.

12

The five colors blind the eye.
The five tones deafen the ear.
The five flavors dull the mouth.

Racing through the field and hunting make the mind wild.
Searching for precious goods leads astray.

Therefore, the sage attends to the belly,
And not to what he sees.
He rejects the latter and chooses the former.

Moderation

This chapter obviously continues the reasoning of the previous one. The 11th chapter's theme of emptiness is followed by this chapter's praise of moderation.

The five colors in the Chinese tradition are green, red, yellow, white, and black. The five tones of the Chinese musical scale are C, D, E, G, and A. The five flavors are sweet, bitter, salty, sour, and pungent.

This division into five is likely to have come from the Chinese concept of the five elements: water, fire, wood, metal, and earth. In ancient China it was believed that everything in the world was made up of these five materials. This can be compared to the old Greek elements, which were four: fire, earth, air, and water.

Lao Tzu warns against any form of excess. A multitude of colors is chaotic, straining for the eyes to watch, and not a pretty sight. Any artist would agree. Similarly, all the instruments in the orchestra playing at once should not go on for long. It works in a crescendo, but rarely elsewhere. A skilled chef limits the number of flavors on a dish, or none of them becomes delightful. Disciplined moderation is a key to great art of whatever genre. Less is more.

This is not only true for art, but for life in general. If we stimulate ourselves with noise, excitement, and hurried action, then our minds start to boil and reason escapes them. There are moments when intensity is unavoidable, maybe also cherished, but they should be few, and there should be generous pauses between them.

Not only does excess of this kind confuse the mind, but it dulls it, too. Adventures lose their appeal when they become routine. Nothing is so exhilarating that we can do it constantly without getting bored. Any thrill needs to be exotic. The more familiar it gets, the less of a thrill it becomes. That's the practical reason for avoiding gluttony of any kind.

Precious objects, no matter how tempting, should not lead our steps. They are just things. If we allow them to control our lives, we are sure to choose paths that have the least to do with what we need. Of true and lasting value is what happens inside of us, so a step towards anything else can only take us farther away from it. A true quest both begins and ends within ourselves. Every other direction is a roundabout.

The Belly

The sage stays within, caring for the needs of his belly instead of striving for what his eyes can see. This refers not only to making sure of getting food, before searching for other delights. In the Eastern tradition, the stomach is regarded as far more than the location of one's intestines. It's the seat of personal resources, even awareness of sorts. The stomach is the center of the human body.

Traditionally, the belly is also the center of personal power. Of course, this is quite accurate from a medical standpoint, since the stomach processes the food and extracts the nutrition and energy we need to survive. The old Chinese teaching also tells us that inside the belly is the major source of the vital breath, the life force *ch'i* (also spelled *qi*). See more about the vital breath in my comments on chapter 10.

According to this tradition, the center of the stomach is *tan t'ien* (also spelled *dantian*), the red rice field, from which great energy emerges. To stimulate the flow of life force within yourself, you need to focus on this center and act according to its impulses.

So, when Lao Tzu says that we should attend to our belly, instead of what our eyes can see, he also means that we should make sure to stay centered. Focusing on the belly keeps you grounded and collected. It's how to guard your integrity and get to know yourself properly. When our eyes trick us to forget what our bellies tell us, our minds get lost and our bodies are sure to suffer.

Lao Tzu reminds us to get our priorities right. In doing so, we get to know ourselves and stay true to what we really are. What the eyes show us may very well be illusions, but what we feel inside our bellies is for real.

13

Praise and disgrace cause fear.
Honor and great distress are like the body.

What does it mean that praise and disgrace cause fear?
Praise leads to weakness.
Getting it causes fear, losing it causes fear.
This is why praise and disgrace cause fear.

What does it mean that honor and great distress are like the body?
The reason for great distress is the body.
Without it, what distress could there be?

Therefore:
He who treasures his body as much as the world
Can care for the world.
He who loves his body as much as the world
Can be entrusted with the world.

Fear

Is there any driving force in man surpassing that of fear? We struggle all our lives to master it, and to avoid anything that brings it about. Fear rules our existence to the extent that there are few things we do without it being one of our reasons, more often than not the most important one.

We worry about not getting what we want, and dread losing what we have. We lock our doors, we arm ourselves, we choose our friends carefully and scrutinize them constantly, we keep strangers off, we fill our everyday lives with numerous precautions, and still we worry about what the future might bring.

Safety first, we say, making our controlled environment a rigidly enclosed area that may keep danger out, but definitely also locks ourselves in. Fleeing from our fear, we make our lives more and more of an imprisonment.

The Fear of Death
What we guard with such mania are our own lives, although death is the inevitable end and it doesn't wait for an invitation. The ultimate fear is that of death. It lies inside every other fear.

The death we fear is that of the body. We know nothing else for certain. Our bodies will cease to function and then decay. What happens next is a mystery to us. So, maybe the fear that clings to us through all our lives is not that of death, but of what it will lead to. We want to keep it off, as long as we can, because we don't want to replace something known with what's totally unknown. At the moment of death, what replaces our bodily existence, if anything?

This is expressed by Hamlet in William Shakespeare's drama, when the prince speaks about being or not being. What makes him hesitate to commit suicide is not the thought of complete annihilation, but the possibility of somehow having his consciousness live on – forever: "To sleep, perchance to dream. Ay, there's the rub. For in that sleep of death, what dreams may come when we have shuffled off this mortal coil must give us pause."

So we guard this mortal coil with desperation. We are obsessed with our bodies. Their demands make us dependent, and their fragility makes us fearful. If our bodies were

K'ung Tzu, Confucius, meets Lao Tzu. Chinese woodprint.

not so precious to us, we would have nothing to protect. There would be few things we would fear losing, because only things of the body can be stripped off of it. Neither praise nor disgrace will stick to us if we don't value the body, the physical entity to which they are connected. The same is true for honor as well as distress.

The body is vulnerable. The more important it is to us, the more vulnerable we will be.

Rule by Caution
Still, Lao Tzu doesn't condemn our dependence on our bodies. We need to know that it is so, but then it can be a fortunate circumstance – especially in the case of rulers. The one who rules his realm with the same care he shows his own body, will not hasten to take risks with it.

He will be hesitant in his rule and consider everything very carefully before taking action. He will tend to inflict on his realm as little as possible. This is exactly how Lao Tzu prefers a ruler to be.

Because he worries about the world around him as much as he worries about his own body, such a ruler will be cautious. Then he will do little harm.

Not only rulers should live by this code, but every one of whatever means. If we treat our surroundings with the same care and love as we have for our own bodies, then we are unlikely to cause trouble or damage.

So, Lao Tzu regards the fear we have as an asset, as long as we are aware of its cause and act accordingly. We should aim to preserve the world as we do our bodies. In that way, fear is a good thing. It keeps us alert and cautious, and it helps us set things in their right perspective.

By one simple question, we can stop ourselves from numerous follies that we might otherwise indulge in unwittingly: Is this worth dying for?

14

Look, it cannot be seen,
So it is called invisible.
Listen, it cannot be heard,
So it is called soundless.
Touch, it cannot be caught,
So it is called elusive.
These three cannot be examined,
So they unite into one.

Above it there is no light,
Below it there is no darkness.
Endlessness beyond description.
It returns to non-existence.
It is called the shapeless shape,
The substance without form.
It is called obscurely evasive.
Meet it and you do not see its beginning,
Follow it and you do not see its end.

Hold on to the ancient Way to master the present,
And to learn the distant beginning.
This is called the unbroken strand of the Way.

Obscure Tao

Now and then Lao Tzu marvels at the splendid mystery of Tao, the Way, portraying it with obvious amazement, as if intoxicated by it. This is one such occasion.

Here, he focuses on its obscurity as well as its infinity.

The latter is the reason for the former. Because Tao has no limit in time or space, it cannot be described, not even perceived.

It's the law out of which the universe emerged. It still rules the world and everything in it. So, nothing comes before or after it. Nothing is outside of its reach.

Because it's the natural law that everything must obey, you need to follow it to manage your life. That's the only way to get some kind of bearing on your life – learning the inner workings of life itself. Then you can avoid futile struggle against the nature of things.

If your path is in accordance with Tao, the Way, you can travel through life with ease. Otherwise, it's bound to take you nowhere.

As you get to know the workings of Tao, you also perceive its role in the world as a whole, all the way back to the moment of its emergence. One thing led to the next, which led to the next. That first thing was Tao, and it's still the fundamental cause to every effect. Tao brought order to chaos, whereby the world was shaped. Without Tao it would return to shapeless chaos.

The unbroken strand is the eternity of Tao, from before the world emerged and forever on. Even if the world would collapse, Tao would remain the principle by which the world could emerge anew. Our world is such that everything perishes. But the laws by which things appear and disappear, including the universe itself, remain undamaged. The unbroken strand is the endless procreation according to the law of Tao.

道德經

15

Ancient masters of excellence had a subtle essence,
And a depth too profound to comprehend.
Because they were impossible to comprehend,
I will try to describe them by their appearance.

Cautious, like crossing a river in the winter.
Wary, as if surrounded by strangers.
Dignified, like a guest.
Yielding, like ice about to melt.
Simple, like uncarved wood.
Open, like a valley.
Obscure, like muddy waters.

Who can wait in stillness while the mud settles?
Who can rest until the moment of action?

He who holds on to the Way seeks no excess.
Since he lacks excess,
He can grow old in no need to be renewed.

Ancient Excellence

In the Eastern tradition as well as many other cultures around the world, the past has been regarded as superior to the present. The ancestors were supposed to be wiser and nobler, their society more advanced, and their lives richer in every way.

Our present Western style society is practically unique in having the reversed perspective, which probably started with the scientific revolution in the 17th century. Through history, the most common sentiment has been that the past was superior, the more distant the better, and the future had little more to offer than decay.

Lao Tzu also supported this view, as can be seen in this chapter. He believed that ancient man was closer to Tao, the Way, and therefore lived a wiser, more harmonious life. As people gradually deviated from Tao, their lives became more chaotic and burdened. He wanted his readers to return to Tao, thereby recreating the blessed world of old.

His perspective was no mystery, considering that the most precious and impressive things around him were preserved from past times. So were the palaces and most glorious works of art, so was agriculture and other skills to make life pleasant, and so were the books written with the most profound wisdom and poetic refinement.

Anyone in the days of Lao Tzu would marvel at the heritage from past centuries, and see few equally great contributions by his own generation. It made sense to regard the past as the golden era.

Imitate the Past
Still, Lao Tzu's intent is not to glorify the past, but to teach the present. He wants his readers to learn from the example of the ancient sages. We may not comprehend their wisdom fully, but when copying their behavior we learn by doing. Behaving wisely promotes wisdom.

Aristotle would have called it *mimesis*, imitation. The ancient Greeks were aware of human learning largely being done by imitation. Children imitate their parents. This is how most of the human knowledge and experience is passed on.

So, what is the behavior of the ancient sages that we should copy? In this and other chapters, Lao Tzu makes it clear: The role model is practically the reverse of splendid royalty. Instead of luxury and elevation, the sage should seek a humble place, simplicity, and calm.

The sage should rather wait than spring into action, not to make shortsighted mistakes. He should be modest, not to provoke envy. He should be thoughtful and cautious even about things that others regard as insignificant. The stronger his power, the softer his use of it.

This way, the sage is close to the nature of Tao, thereby understanding its workings. It's the Way of living close to nature, or more precisely: close to the natural.

These days, we seem to seek the very opposite. We long for fame and glory, but forget that the more this is bestowed on us, the less the chances are that we can prove worthy of it. Others will not praise us in their hearts, but say: "That could just as well be me."

A society that glorifies some of its citizens promotes envy, competition, and calamity – unfortunately also stupidity. If we make superficial things our quests, we only find what we searched for, which is superficiality. To reach the profound, we must do away with distractions of that kind. Otherwise the mud never settles, and we never see clearly.

The ancient masters, according to Lao Tzu, knew to renounce nonsense, until only the essence remained. Nowadays, we are probably farther from that than ever before. In that sense, Lao Tzu might be right about the golden era of mankind being in the distant past.

16

Attain utmost emptiness.
Abide in steadfast stillness.

All things arise in unison.
Thereby we see their return.
All things flourish,
And each returns to its source.

Returning to the source is stillness.
It is returning to one's fate.
Returning to one's fate is eternal.
Knowledge of the eternal is realization.

Not knowing of the eternal leads to unfortunate errors.
Knowledge of the eternal is all-embracing.
To be all-embracing leads to righteousness,
Which is majestic.
To be majestic leads to the Heavenly.
To be Heavenly leads to the Way.

The Way is eternal.
Until your last day, you are free from peril.

The Cycle of Life

The universe is cyclic. Celestial bodies move in their strict orbits. On Earth we see the four seasons repeated endlessly. Other repetitions are the moon's monthly phases and the daily shift from sunrise to sunset. All living things are born, grow to maturity, and then pass away. This is the nature of things, whether we approve or not.

Lao Tzu has no doubt that we should appreciate this, not only to be able to come to peace with it, but also so that we understand it. When we accept the cycle of life, we learn something about its patterns and the law that rules it all. That law is Tao, the Way. So, by recognizing the inevitable cycle of existence we are able to perceive and comprehend Tao.

The empty stillness, of which Lao Tzu speaks in the first lines of this chapter, reminds us again of Zen. No doubt, he thinks of some kind of meditation, a pensive mood in which the cycles of life become clear. When you relax from your daily strife, you can notice the patterns of the world around you. You become aware of it all, because you reduce your own inner noise.

Only when we see the cyclic nature of the whole world and all its living things, can we come to terms with the fact that this is inevitably true for ourselves as well. Each of us is bound by the cycle. None can escape it. Solace lies in the fact that we all share this basic fate, and that it goes on infinitely. So, although every single creature in the world has a limited life span, the world as a whole does not. In that sense we are all eternal, because we are part of it all.

When we are aware of this, we learn to appreciate the time we have, and we don't embark on futile attempts to become immortal in one way or other. We should not strive to be glorified by posterity, since that's an illusion of little meaning, making no difference to us at present. Instead, our contribution should simply aim at the present – the world we are in, instead of the world yet to come.

It's also the only way of serving the future properly.

Living in the present, indifferent to what imprint it might make on the future, is to remain with Tao. That calms the mind and invigorates the body. Also, it keeps us out of unnecessary trouble or hardship.

17

The supreme rulers are hardly known by their subjects.
The lesser are loved and praised.
The even lesser are feared.
The least are despised.

Those who show no trust will not be trusted.
Those who are quiet value the words.
When their task is completed, people will say:
We did it ourselves.

Unnoticed Ruler

History has taught us that noisy rulers usually ravage the country. Still, we tend to fall for them when they rise. We should always look for modesty in our leaders, and moderation in their use of power. Those who seek triumph are indifferent to what they need to trample on in order to reach it.

Nowadays, we have a chance to elect our leaders by voting. We don't always have excellent candidates to choose between, but we are still much better off than those countless past generations stuck with kings whose only merit was that they were sons of kings. Inheriting power rarely breeds the proper respect for it.

Lao Tzu gives a clear order of leadership qualities. The same ladder can be used as an indicator of how those leaders safeguard their position.

The most prominent leaders are satisfied to do their work without receiving any praise for it. They don't even care if they are known, or if they will be remembered after their time in office.

The leaders with slightly less prominence make sure that they are loved and appreciated. That's far less noble, but it's still a kind of guarantee that they will do their best to please the people they rule, and protect the land they control. Only benevolence inspires love, and only a job well done wins praise.

Much worse are the leaders who guard their power by threats and force, scaring people into submission. Unfortunately, this is not that difficult, history shows us. So, such leaders are not rare, and they tend to remain in power for far too long. Fear, as Lao Tzu has already explained above, is everywhere.

So, it's easy to find and to stimulate. Those who want to indulge in power tend to prefer it, because it makes their power evident as well as impressive. But such power is fragile, since those ruled by it only wish for it to end.

Feared leaders are still not the worst, Lao Tzu tells us. Such leaders can still be admired, and people are excused for not revolting.

The worst ones are despised, having no merit in the eyes of their people. This is worse than fear, because it's shameful – for the leader, and even more so for those he leads, since they allow themselves to be ruled by someone they cannot respect. It's a reign of disgrace, which risks leading even the most splendid country into decay.

Any Leader
What Lao Tzu says about rulers is true also for all kinds of leaders further down in the hierarchy. A boss doesn't have to be big to be bad – or good. As soon as someone has the

least bit of power over other people, no matter how few they are, the above applies.

Competent rulers are trusted, and trust that they receive this trust. Otherwise they feel the need to ascertain their power by other means. But trust is such that it neither grows nor remains if it's not mutual. The one who shows trust expects to get it in return, so those who want it must also give it.

If a trusted leader shows no trust in the people he leads, then soon enough their trust in him will vanish. Rightly so. Someone who expects the worst from others is likely to accept it in himself. He may even use his suspicions to justify his own malice, calling it precaution or a preemptive strike. Distrust poisons society much quicker than blind faith ever does.

Words should be used with the same moderation as power. A leader arguing his case abundantly is probably trying to cover its weakness. Rhetoric can be as fine as poetry, but it says very little about the issue at hand. Words are not deeds, so words about deeds give no guarantee as to how they will turn out. This is evident in modern politics, where passionate speeches are a dime a dozen, but still most problems wait for their solutions.

We would say that action speaks louder than words, but Lao Tzu was no friend of noise. He would rather have the action so discreet that it passed unnoticed, and therefore no words at all were needed.

18

When the great Tao is abandoned,
Benevolence and righteousness arise.
When wisdom and knowledge appear,
Great pretense arises.
When family ties are disturbed,
Devoted children arise.
When people are unsettled,
Loyal ministers arise.

Pretense

Tao is the Way of the universe. If we just follow it, there is no risk of going wrong. But when we deviate from it, we are sure to make mistakes, no matter how noble our intentions are. Following Tao is doing what is natural. Anything else is a mistake, leading to complications, shortcomings, and confusion.

Benevolence and righteousness are fine qualities, but they are no guarantee of doing the right thing. If our loss of the Way is substituted by ever so good intentions, they are still just substitutes. Using them as compasses for our actions is bound to lead us even more astray. Our good deeds turn out to have bad consequences, because they lack the understanding of how things work at length in this world.

Lao Tzu was no friend of knowledge and wisdom. He saw them as meager substitutes for a true understanding of Tao and sincere acceptance of its terms. At the Chinese emperor's court, he had seen wise men use their wisdom for their own advancement. They played their roles with cunning and cleverness, but rarely used their mental resources for the benefit of all.

Even when used with the best intentions, knowledge is a poor guide, compared to awareness of Tao. It creates a false understanding of the world. Therefore it leads to false conclusions. Anyone wise enough to recognize this has the choice of either throwing it all away in search of Tao, or insisting on knowledge being a perfectly reliable substitute. The latter takes some folly to trust.

There is pretense in claiming that wisdom finds the Way, and there is pretense in claiming that knowledge penetrates Tao. They are insufficient substitutes, no matter how pompously they present themselves.

The family ties are sacred in China, as well as in most societies around the world. The Confucian tradition describes those ties as duties. Lao Tzu implies that they are natural, as is shown among animals. There is no debate involved in it, nor should rules be at all necessary. But when Tao is lost, so are the natural family ties.

If the children still remain devoted to their parents, there seems to be no need for complaint. But this devotion is odd and flawed. There are conditions, from the children towards the parents as well as the other way around, even when the bonds seem unreserved. Parents have expectations on their children, and children have demands on their parents. Devotion is a contract that usually contains a lot of fine print.

In that way, devotion can be compared to pretense.

Fragile Loyalty
Another kind of pretense is that of loyal ministers. Their loyalty is always conditional, mainly in the sense that it's given to the one in power at the moment. A ruler who loses

power will instantly lose the loyalty of the ministers, who move on to praise whoever sits on the throne next.

When people are unsettled, changes in government are more likely to take place. That makes the ministers more eager to demonstrate their loyalty, in order to keep their own positions in the turmoil, but their loyalty is actually less trustworthy in such a situation. The ministers who proclaim their loyalty the loudest, are the most likely to shift at the moment it's to their benefit.

If the people is unsettled, it means that the country is in some kind of turmoil. The former order of things is no longer the case, at least not to the extent that people can rely on it. This is indeed a country far from Tao, the natural order of things.

When Tao rules, there's no struggle over leadership. That starts at the moment the country loses its calm. Then, ministers and other officials will suddenly appear all over the palace, assuring the ruler how loyal they are. This is nothing but a sign of unrest, and the ruler who doesn't regard such loyalty with the utmost suspicion and wariness will not stay in power for long.

19

Abandon wisdom, discard knowledge,
And people will benefit a hundredfold.
Abandon benevolence, discard duty,
And people will return to the family ties.
Abandon cleverness, discard profit,
And thieves and robbers will disappear.

These three, though, are superficial, and not enough.
Let this be what to rely on:

Behave simply and hold on to purity.
Lessen selfishness and restrain desires.
Abandon knowledge and your worries are over.

Gain by Abandoning

This chapter clearly continues the thoughts of the previous one. Lao Tzu made no division of his text into chapters. That came much later. It may very well be so that Lao Tzu intended these two chapters to be read as one. Either that or the previous chapter simply inspired the next.

The topic of this 19th chapter is how to avoid the misfortune pointed out in chapter 18. When Tao, the Way, is abandoned, all kinds of miseries arrive. It's better to abandon everything but Tao. Then the only thing remaining will be clear to everybody.

Letting go of things that society generally appreciates is the way of the monk, the elevated and spiritual human being. That's the message in just about any philosophy and religion. It's at the core of Zen, which comes very close to what the *Tao Te Ching* preaches.

Lao Tzu gives solid reasons for why we should abandon all these things.

Too Much to Know
Wisdom and knowledge confuse people. The more they are exposed to it, the less they are able to understand about life, and the likelier they are to lose their direction. The wisdom that is extracted from knowledge quickly becomes cryptic, and knowledge in any quantity leaves most people uncertain, fearful of what they may need to grasp.

Today, we certainly live in a society that praises knowledge, maybe more than ever before in history. That's because we have so much more of it, nowadays. The sum of human knowledge is said to double every five years. That surely depends on how it's calculated, but there is no doubt that we have gathered far more knowledge than anyone can learn in a lifetime.

It means that no matter how hard we try, there will always be much more we don't know than what we know. An endless race, where we are left farther and farther behind.

Also the wisest of our time are entangled in this growing web of knowledge, making them doubt their own conclusions and therefore reluctant to reach them at all. We can't see the forest for all the trees. The more we know, the less we are sure to understand.

Knowledge has its own procreation. The more we learn, the more there is yet to learn. There is no wisdom that can penetrate this, so knowledge exceeding our brain capacity lessens our ability to treat it wisely.

There are countless examples in our society of when

knowledge makes us jump to conclusions of little sense. We hang on to them because we believe that facts make reason obsolete. But knowledge needs to be filtered and tried by reason, not to be misunderstood.

We gather such quantities of facts that we have no time to consider what to make of them. Instead, we hurry to conclusions, which are soon replaced by new conclusions, and so on. The more we know, the less we can trust that this knowledge will not be contradicted by future knowledge.

Nothing is certain for long in this flood of facts. We had better hold on to common sense.

The Malice of Benevolence

Lao Tzu also argues that we should abandon benevolence. This seems odd from a writer who is obviously compassionate. But what he sees is that benevolence and duty replace the natural care shown within families and other relations between people.

There's no need for a written or unwritten law about care, since that comes to us instinctually. Parents protect their children and children are forever fond of their parents. We don't need morals or rules for this. If duty is imposed, what would have come naturally becomes a burden that people try to avoid. The same, although to a lesser extent, can be said about benevolence if it's expected of people, because then it becomes a duty.

There is also another unwanted side of benevolence. It breeds dependence, and in some cases it carries an ingredient of contempt. The benevolent make themselves superior, as if acting from above. Therefore, it's better to stick to what can be called good will among men.

The benevolent interfere, sometimes more than what is

called for. With mutual respect we find how to do the most good by doing less.

No Love
There is nothing said about love in the *Tao Te Ching*. This sentiment, as we in the Western tradition know it, is kind of strange to the old Eastern mind. We fall in love and form loving ties to one another, but to Lao Tzu and many other Chinese thinkers, this bond is better described by other words.

When Lao Tzu tells us to trust our family ties instead of benevolence or duty, he hints on the quality that we prefer to call love. He would probably find more sense in calling it compassion. Love tends to exclude more than it includes. And there is always a danger that it leads to hatred towards the ones not embraced by it. We should not reserve our good deeds only for those we love.

As pointed out at the end of this chapter, we should avoid selfishness and control our desires. Love tends to do the opposite. So, although Lao Tzu is most definitely compassionate, he is no advocate of love as a ruler of our action.

The last line of the chapter, "Abandon knowledge and your worries are over," is in many versions of the *Tao Te Ching* placed as the first line of chapter 20. Although this is supported somewhat by several old manuscripts, there are still far more arguments for putting the line here, where its content and form make so much more sense than it would in the next chapter, which deals with other things entirely.

It made little difference to Lao Tzu, since he had no division into chapters at all. The proper way of reading the *Tao Te Ching* is from beginning to end, without pause.

20

What's the difference between yes and no?
What's the difference between beautiful and ugly?
Must one dread what others dread?
Oh barbarity! Will it never end?

Other people are joyous, like on the feast of the ox,
Like on the way up to the terrace in the spring.
I alone am inert, giving no sign,
Like a newborn baby who has not learned to smile.
I am wearied, as if I lacked a home to go to.

Other people have more than they need,
I alone seem wanting.
I have the mind of a fool,
Understanding nothing.

The common people see clearly,
I alone am held in the dark.
The common people are sharp,
Only I am clumsy,
Like drifting on the waves of the sea,
Without direction.

Other people are occupied,
I alone am unwilling, like the outcast.
I alone am different from the others,
Because I am nourished by the great mother.

I Am Alone

In this the 20th chapter, Lao Tzu's tone suddenly changes. It gets personal, which is very rare in the *Tao Te Ching*. There is even something close to anguish showing. He watches people enjoy themselves in their ignorance, while he is unattached. Therefore, his soul finds no immediate gratification.

The personal tone has made researchers question the authenticity of this and similar parts of the book.

In the oldest known manuscript (from Guodian, c. 300 BC), all the lines of this personal nature are missing – from "Oh barbarity!" and down.

In the two next to oldest versions (from Mawangdui, around 200 BC), though, the lines are present. This suggests that they have been added in this period. If so, it was probably done by a commentator reflecting on the text while copying it.

But one single manuscript of old is not conclusive. It's just as likely that the copier of the Guodian manuscript skipped these lines for some reason. That manuscript is far from complete.

In any case, the text as a whole is definitely written with both mind and heart, so personal reflections are not out of context. Human folly is a recurring theme, and this chapter is more about that than about the author's frustration – although the latter can come as no surprise.

So, whether it's written by Lao Tzu or somebody sympathizing with him, doesn't make that much of a difference. I have no problem believing that Lao Tzu, in the process of writing his text of 5000 words, had occasional outbursts of grief, frustration – even desperation. The world he studied was his own habitat, so how could he not react to his findings about it?

Uncertainties

There are other uncertainties about this chapter. In many versions of the *Tao Te Ching*, it starts with what is here the last line of chapter 19: "Abandon knowledge and your worries are over." Most researchers into the text would agree with my choice, for several obvious reasons.

It must be remembered that the text was originally written without any division into chapters. That was introduced several centuries later. Lao Tzu's text should really be read as a flowing continuum from a mind eager to get it all out. This is shown by how the themes evolve and get treated, one after the other. It's also hinted by the rhythm of repetitions, and the manner in which some themes return later on in the text.

Tao Te Ching gives a strong impression of being written by one person, who allowed ideas that appeared during the writing of one line to lead to the next. The same seems to be the case with the themes treated. The structure of the whole text is more like a river floating through a changing landscape, than a building raised according to plan. There is spontaneity, and order is found more in each part than in the whole.

With this in mind, the last line of chapter 19 makes more sense there, than as a start of chapter 20.

Actually, the book should probably be divided into significantly more than 81 chapters, judging from its content. The number of chapters was decided for symbolic reasons, creating the symmetry of 9 X 9.

This leads to several oddities in the chapters. Some of

Lao Tzu riding out of China on a water buffalo. This is the most common Lao Tzu motif. Here, he holds a copy of the Tao Te Ching. Ink painting by Chang Lu, 16th century.

道德經 107

them start off with one subject, then suddenly switch to another, changing form and rhyme patterns accordingly.

That's evident in this chapter, where the first four lines differ from the following ones. True, they form what can be seen as an introduction to what follows, but they could very well also be seen as a chapter in its own right. This is even more obvious in several other cases.

Finally, regarding this chapter, the second line does in most versions of the text read: "What's the difference between good and bad?" But the oldest known manuscripts, the two discovered in Mawangdui in the 1970's and the one found in Guodian in the 1990's, all say "beautiful and ugly" instead.

The difference is not that great. Good and bad should not be understood in a strictly moral way, but similarly to pleasing and displeasing, whereas beautiful and ugly must be understood as something other than mere facial value.

I have chosen the latter, because the oldest manuscripts support it, and because it connects to the thoughts about opposites presented in the second chapter.

Fear

The chapter starts with the questioning of polarities that can be recognized from earlier chapters. Are opposites really that different? Then Lao Tzu asks if we must dread what others dread. He seems to imply that judgments on what is preferable or not in society are based on fear. If so, this is in accordance with a lot of modern thinking.

Upon examination, mankind is revealed to make many of its decisions – as individuals as well as groups – based on fear. In particular, many of our very worst decisions have that ingredient.

Personal fear is treated in chapter 13, but the dread Lao Tzu mentions here is more of a social one. People foster prejudice about what is acceptable and what is not. Fear lurks inside this prejudice.

Surely, the ancient time when Lao Tzu walked the earth was no different from ours in how people hurried to live as they believed was expected of them, and cursed anything else without a moment of consideration.

Man is a social beast, and that urge in us often leads to beastly behavior. This is especially true as soon as fear is somehow involved – fear of the unknown, fear of anything different, fear of not conforming. We foster a lot of fears.

Being Different
One of the things that people in just about any society fear the most is being different, which is exactly what Lao Tzu concludes that he is. Others live their lives, seemingly without a care in the world, but Lao Tzu is unable to participate. He is an outsider, and the reason for this is his insight into the true nature of existence.

What he has discovered sets him so much apart from all the others that he is unable to play along with them. He is utterly alone, but not without pride. In the last line he concludes that what sets him apart is the fact that he lives by Tao, the Way.

He may lack a human family to embrace, but his mother is the very law and creator of the universe.

So, this outcast has cast himself out. Lao Tzu's isolation is a result of the path he has chosen. He could not do differently, without denying what he had come to realize about life. Although his isolation is a high price to pay, denying his findings would be even more costly to him.

That is, as they say, a hard act to follow. But it's not unique. People who stand by their ideals and convictions experience it, and through history there are countless souls who have paid for it with their lives.

Not all of them nourished beliefs with which we would agree. Some of them even fought for things that we have for good reasons come to condemn. But the mechanism of exclusion from society is much the same, whether people leave their fellow men to pursue the path of truth or that of deception. In any case, they are themselves the last to know.

This is the fate of fanatics, but to some extent it's true for each and every one of us. In the core of our hearts, we are all alone.

Our fear of standing out stems mostly from the suspicion that we actually are different from everybody else, which is something we struggle frantically to hide.

It's a strange thing. If we could stop and observe the desperate loneliness in the depth of everybody else's eyes, maybe we could finally grow out of this the most superfluous of fears. That single discovery would bless mankind more than any other I can think of.

Probably, we would at that moment discover that we are all doing the same as Lao Tzu – nourishing from the great mother, and following her course.

21

The greatest virtue is to follow the Way utterly.
Its nature is utterly vague and evasive.
How evasive and vague!
Yet its center has form.
How vague and evasive!
Yet its center has substance.
How deep and obscure!
Yet its center has essence.
This essence is real,
So, its center can be trusted.

From now back to antiquity,
Its name has not been lost.
Thereby, see the origin of all.
How do I know it is the origin of all?
By this.

The Clarity of Obscurity

This is an outburst of the poet in Lao Tzu. Here and in many other chapters of the book, he suddenly marvels at the magnificent mystery of it all. But it's not a mystery in which he is lost or blinded. Quite the opposite.

Because he dares to face the mystery in all its obscurity, it becomes clear to him.

He doesn't mind the darkness, since he is quite aware of what it hides. The evasiveness doesn't make him doubt, since he has already understood. Instead, he sees this evasiveness and darkness as evidence of the profundity. Anything less profound would be easier to perceive and to comprehend.

Tao, the Way, is primordial. Not only was it present at the very birth of the world, but it was the actual origin out of which the world emerged. Its own origin, if there is one, is the most distant of all.

So, Tao must be obscure, evasive, and vague. Anything by which to describe Tao is of later date and lesser significance, so Tao remains forever impenetrable. Its nature may be grasped intuitively, but not explained.

That's the elusive character of many truly profound things in life, in art, and in science. What we easily express in a few sentences is unlikely to penetrate the surface. Once we really dig deep into what we examine, the truth becomes more and more absurd, and less possible to convey to those who remain on the surface.

During the 20th century, natural science revealed a lot of such absurdities, and found them to be core components of the whole universe.

Astronomy has taught us that the cosmos is not eternal in its width, but still impossible to exit, and its vastness was born out of a single point, a center with minimal volume but unfathomable density.

Einstein proved that time is not a constant. Much to his frustration, quantum physics discovered that the smallest pieces of matter refuse inspection, since they are affected by our scrutiny.

Not to mention string theory, yet to be accepted, where the building blocks of the universe seem to be dancing.

The universe appears to be described quite accurately, although obscurely, by the words of Lao Tzu.

The Center of Tao

Lao Tzu speaks repeatedly about the center of Tao, as if it would differ from its periphery or anything in between. But Tao is the very law of nature, so it contains no differences or discrepancies. Otherwise there would be anomalies and exceptions in the way the universe works. It would collapse, as would Tao.

What Lao Tzu refers to is the difference between the outside view, when Tao is observed by those who don't comprehend it, and what its true nature really is.

The latter can be called its center. The actual word used also means middle, as in the Chinese name of the country: the Middle Kingdom. That name stems from an old belief – or aspiration – of being the country in the middle of the world, as if China were its very axis.

Lao Tzu expresses no such belief about the country he served before leaving to write his book, but when he points to the origin of all, he has to go to the middle. Neither in his understanding of the world, nor in modern astronomical theory, is it possible for a universe to appear from anywhere else than its middle, its center. Nothing can appear from its own periphery.

So, when Lao Tzu speaks of the center of Tao, he speaks of that which was the origin of the whole world.

In that way, Tao has form because of all the forms being born out of it, and it has substance through all the matter that came out of it, filling the world. It also has essence, which is its creative force, its active presence. Without that essence, no world would have emerged. Tao would only have been an eternal possibility, resting in its own perfection.

The essence of Tao is similar to the expressed will of the

Bible's God, uttering: "Let there be..." Tao may have no similarly traceable intention, but the result is the same. The universe was born, because that event was in the nature of Tao.

By What?

The chapter ends with a mysterious remark: "By this." Surely, this is Lao Tzu's humor at play. How else to end a chapter about the mysterious nature of Tao?

The word Tao was known long before the days of Lao Tzu, and this he was certainly aware of. So were his expected readers. Tao and its complex meaning can be seen in texts and traditions dating so far back from the days of Lao Tzu that he would probably have had no idea of their origin in time. So, on that very concrete level, he uses the well-known antiquity of the word Tao as an argument for why it must describe the very origin of all.

Tao was known in cosmological speculations of Lao Tzu's time, and the time before his. *T'ien chih Tao*, Heaven's Way, was used in descriptions of the divine and other things beyond human understanding. Lao Tzu would not have caused any uproar in the Chinese minds of his time, when stating that the great antiquity of the word Tao was evidence of its cosmic significance.

But his comment has several levels. He is also likely to refer to the elusive obscurity of Tao. Something as vague and incomprehensible must be of fundamental importance and dignity. What man cannot comprehend is of divine nature. If it were easier to grasp, it would not be as elevated. In that way, the mystery of Tao is a sign of its greatness.

In all cultures of old, what was not understood was regarded as divine or Heavenly, belonging to a greater realm than that of human existence. The many wonders in nature were seen as indications of a great order of things, governed elsewhere by other forces than those that humans and animals had at their disposal. Whether those forces were in the hands of gods of some sort or not, they were definitely out of human reach.

Not only were humans unable to copy those feats, but also to understand them. Ancient man made little difference between the two. These inabilities were the two sides of the same coin. What could not be understood could not be done, and what could not be done could not be understood.

In a way, this is still true, although we have all kinds of explanations – but not to the very core, the center of the workings of the universe. Some natural laws we can utilize to our advantage, and some processes in nature we can copy for our own benefit. But we lack certainty as to what really makes everything work, at the very bottom – what Lao Tzu calls the center. Our sciences are sketch works, where closer inspection shows that many details are still missing. Our lines have not connected all the dots.

Mostly, we lack the knowledge that makes sense to it all. The unified field theory that Einstein dreamed about is still outside our grasp. So is the exact state the universe was in, before its Big Bang. Like Lao Tzu, when we look at the beginning we see the mystery. It can be named, but not explained.

We know that it has to be there, since we can observe its surroundings, to which we do ourselves belong. But we have yet to reach it.

22

Hulk to be whole.
Bend to be straight.
Empty to be filled.
Wear down to be renewed.
Reduce to gain.
Excess confuses.

Therefore, the sage embraces the one,
And is an example to the world.
He does not show off, therefore he shines.
He does not justify himself, therefore he is revered.
He does not boast, therefore he is honored.
He does not praise himself, therefore he remains.
Because he opposes no one,
No one in the world can oppose him.

The ancients said:
Hulk to be whole.
Are these just empty words?
Indeed, he shall remain whole.

Humility Brings Honor

"Blessed are the meek," said Jesus, and continued: "for they will inherit the earth." That's also Lao Tzu's message in this chapter. Humility is praised, whereas its opposite meets with protests and contempt.

It's not a question of envy. We can live with the success of others, even congratulate them wholeheartedly. But not

The Tao sign in three old versions (bronze, big seal, and seal), and in its present form.

if they brag. We accept that other people have power over our lives, but not if they are rude. We need to feel that privileged people are worthy of their privileges. At least, we don't want them to be unworthy. That upsets us.

We expect life and civilization to have some kind of built-in justice. That may be naïve, stemming from the morals of fairy tales, myths, and legends. It's also the principle applied to just about every Hollywood movie. We would loathe a movie ending with the villain being victorious at the cost of our hero.

Aristotle pointed it out in *The Poetics*, his text on the rules of drama. The audience can come to terms with the good and virtuous meeting a tragic end, but not with the bad and immoral achieving final success. It would upset and disgust us. Every playwright since before Aristotle's time has been aware of this, so a drama ending in conflict with this principle is mighty hard to find.

We would really like life to be the same. So, whenever we have the chance, we act to make it so. We hurry to condemn people who don't behave nobly in their splendor, and we take any chance to strip them of their privileges. Even kings can fall, when confronted with this power of the people.

The only thing they have to do in order for us to accept

their good fortune is to be modest about it. Then we congratulate them.

To Lao Tzu, this is more than a necessity to avoid provoking others. It's in accordance with nature and the principle of Tao. The universal world order of Tao is meek. It acts in a submissive way, but still it rules the universe. The world is run by yielding principles, so we must do the same in order to succeed with our intentions.

We might not always be successful when walking this path, but we are sure to fail miserably if we choose the opposite direction. Neither mankind nor nature will comply.

23

To be of few words is natural.

Strong winds do not last all morning,
Hard rains do not last all day.
What cause them?
Heaven and Earth.
If Heaven and Earth are unable to persist,
How could man?

Those who follow the Way are one with the Way.
Those who live virtuously are one with virtue.
Those who deprive themselves are one with deprivation.

Those who are one with the Way are welcomed by the Way.
Those who are one with virtue are welcomed by virtue.
Those who are one with deprivation are deprived of deprivation.

Those who do not show trust will not be trusted.

Deprived of Deprivation

Greed and excess are not kindly treated by nature. Every culture contains several examples of this in myths, fables, and historical records. Lao Tzu states it several times in his book. Here, he also points out that sacrifice brings its very own form of reward: Those who are willing to make sacrifices will often find that they avoid them. They are deprived of deprivation.

Lao Tzu plays with words, but not with their meaning.

The nature of deprivation is such that those who welcome it will be deprived of it. Deprivation ignores them. Their sacrifice is not called for, just because they willingly offer it.

This also means that those who try to avoid it will get it in abundance. What you try to escape is exactly what will hunt you, like the predator does its prey. Living is not for free. Those who try to escape the costs will be charged double and triple, whereas those who willingly open their purse will find it untouched. The major costs in life appear for those who reject them.

There is what we call poetic justice to life. From those who take indiscriminately, there will be taken. To those who give willingly, there will be given. Life is a puzzle of paradoxes, making sense only at a distance.

So, when Lao Tzu concludes in the last line, which seems to be only vaguely connected to this chapter, that you must show trust to be trusted, then he means it to be true also for your relation to nature and its Way. Those who volunteer to make sacrifices have that trust, and therefore the Way of nature goes their way.

It's easier said than done, but accepting life as it unfolds in front of you is the most rewarding way through it.

24

Those who stand on their toes are not steady.
Those who take long steps cannot keep the pace.
Those who show off do not shine.
Those who are self-righteous are not prominent.
Those who boast are not respected.
Those who praise themselves do not prevail.

To the Way,
Such people are surplus provisions and useless actions.
They are rejected by many.
Therefore:
Those who follow the Way do not remain with them.

Banned If You Boast

The world is full of self-appointed stars. I have a hard time condemning such people, partly because I might be one of them and partly because it's quite understandable, considering the short rat race we have entered by no will of our own.

To put it bluntly, we are all going to die, and we know it. That's not a very envious position to be in. So, we try to make the best of it in any way we can. We're quite desperate to make it meaningful and significant. Right there is where false pride, self-righteousness, and bragging begin. It's understandable. How else to keep a brave heart as death inevitably approaches?

Still, Lao Tzu is not wrong. If we allow this bragging and self-appraisal to clog what we see in the mirror, then we are sure to be victims of contempt. The reason is simple. We all share the same insoluble dilemma – a life always somehow too short, with an inescapable end at an unpredictable moment. Since that's the burden we all carry, who is to stand out, who is to wear a crown and sit on a throne?

The only way to show respect towards all the others sharing the same predicament is to be humble about it.

There are many who offend the guidelines of this chapter in the *Tao Te Ching*. Honestly, don't we all, occasionally? Some do it on a regular basis and with a vengeance. In many cases, they have admirers who assist them in this worship. Actually, we seem to love having idols that we praise for a while, and then forget or condemn.

It's our longing for a life full of meaning. If we can't all have it, let's choose some of us to laureate, in order to keep the dream alive. These idols of ours are also our victims. Like the chosen ones among the pre-Columbian Chichimecas, our idols are cheered and spoiled for a time, and then sacrificed. Whether the praise is just one's own or shared by one's fellow men, the outcome is equally costly.

We want to survive death, somehow. We want to make a mark. That aspiration is one of envy of the gods of our own invention. We want to be them. The old Greeks called it *hubris*, comparing oneself to the gods. We would call it delusion. It's not folly, but solace against the sad facts of life. We need to rid ourselves of the sadness by which we regard our fate, in order to overcome it.

That's no easy path, but Lao Tzu also informs us that nobody said it was going to be easy. Tao might be the Way to a life of ease, in accordance with the universe, but getting there is no picnic.

25

There was something that finished chaos,
Born before Heaven and Earth.
So silent and still!
So pure and deep!
It stands alone and immutable,
Ever-present and inexhaustible.
It can be called the mother of the whole world.
I do not know its name. I call it the Way.
For the lack of better words I call it great.

Great means constant flow.
Constant flow means far-reaching.
Far-reaching means returning.

That is how the Way is great.
Heaven is great,
Earth is great,
And the king is also great.
In the world there are four greats,
And the king is one of them.

Man is ruled by Earth.
Earth is ruled by Heaven.
Heaven is ruled by the Way.
The Way is ruled by itself.

Four Greats

Not once, but twice, Lao Tzu states that the king is one of the greats – as if he struggles to convince himself of it. He was obviously not unaware of possible doubts to this statement.

There have been some kings through the ages who would have been better described with completely different words. Surely, China in the distant past of Lao Tzu had already experienced a few. He would need to say it twice to make sure that his readers didn't brush it aside as mere irony.

But Lao Tzu doesn't speak of individual kings, men who have upheld the position with honor or disgrace. He speaks about ruling as such, a power as necessary as the other three to ward off chaos. Later in this book he gives many clues as to how he means the king should behave, thereby implying that it's far from always the case, but he is equally clear about the need for a king, a ruler, for civilization not to perish. Even a bad ruler is better than no ruler at all, although sometimes it's far from obvious.

By repeating his statement about the king, Lao Tzu hints the daring thought of actually contemplating the question: Would we be better off without one? His answer is no, but with little enthusiasm, since he is well aware of royal shortcomings. Man is an erring creature, and with a crown on his head it can lead to disaster. Still, if no one wears it, mayhem is certain. That's a consequence of how the universe is ordered according to Tao, the Way.

In the days of the mighty autocratic kings of Europe, they were said to have their power from God. Lao Tzu seems to imply something similar with his descending

混 *Hun, chaos.*

chain, from Tao through Heaven and Earth to the king, as if the king had his authority from the higher greats. But neither Tao nor Heaven or Earth are gods. They are entities making up the universe by staying in their places and upholding their functions. That's what the king should do, as well.

Otherwise, there would be a return to the chaos that existed before the world was formed out of the principle of Tao.

Chaos

The Chinese word used for chaos, *hun*, means mixed, mingled, and confused. It describes a state where nothing is separated from the rest, a primordial mud of everything. This is also what the Greek concept chaos originally stands for.

The Chinese pictogram combines the signs for water, the sun, and the word same: water and the sun are the same. When not even the sun and the water are separable, there is chaos indeed. Such a primordial chaos is common in creation myths around the world. Usually, it's seen as a dark primordial sea. This is the case also in the first book of Genesis in the Bible.

Today, we tend to use the word chaos differently, describing a bundle of things or events in no order. But the original idea of chaos is a homogenous mass, a single entity out of which nothing has yet been formed.

To Lao Tzu, this primordial singularity was only preceded by Tao, the principle by which the chaos was later divided into all things. The calmness of that principle, before setting things into motion, is what Lao Tzu praises in the beginning of this chapter, as if he is almost longing back to it.

Out of this primordial chaos and by the principle of Tao, Heaven, Earth, and all other things appeared. Creation and procreation. That's how Tao is constantly flowing, far-reaching, and returning. Creation is constantly taking place, as all things appear, wither, and disappear, later to reappear in other shapes.

26

Heavy is the root of light.
Stillness is the ruler of haste.

Therefore:
Although he travels all day,
The sage never loses sight of his luggage carts.
Only when he rests securely inside the walls,
He relaxes his attention.

Why would a ruler with ten thousand chariots
Look lightly on himself or his domain?
In lightness the root is lost.
In haste the ruler is lost.

Be Still

In his stream of wisdom, Lao Tzu also occasionally enjoys playing with words. He does so in the very first lines of the *Tao Te Ching*, where Tao is used as both a noun and a verb. In this chapter, the joke is the ruler in the second line compared to the last line.

In the former, the principle of stillness is the ruler of haste, whereas in the last line the ruler who is lost in haste is a human one, neglecting himself and his domain.

It's a high-brow kind of humor, one would say, but Lao Tzu might have giggled putting it together. The book has several examples of the same kind of humor, a play with words that creates double meanings – both of them profound. That's what many poets can't resist doing.

To be heavy is shouldering one's responsibilities and holding one's ground. Stillness is acting with caution and well prepared. This is important for anyone to understand, but particularly for a ruler, since the consequences of neglect would be much direr.

We have just learned, in chapter 25, that the king is one of the four greats, so he has to behave like one. Power means responsibility and responsibility means care. The ruler has the most in his care, so he has to be the most careful.

Being heavy and still, a ruler does not eagerly spring into action, but waits until it is time, and then does just what is called for. Nothing more.

Eagerness to act tends to create more problems than it solves.

27

A good wanderer leaves no trace.
A good speaker does not stutter.
A good counter needs no calculator.
A good door needs no lock,
Still it can't be opened.
A good mooring needs no knot,
Still no one can untie it.

Therefore the sage takes care of all people,
Forsaking no one.
He takes care of all things,
Forsaking nothing.
This is called following the light.

So, a good person is the bad person's teacher.
A bad person is the good person's task.
The one who does not honor the teacher
And the one who does not honor the task,
Although ever so knowledgeable,
They are confused.
This is called the subtle essence.

Teacher and Student

The Eastern tradition is essentially focused on transmitting the wisdom of old to the coming generations. Everybody is primarily a student and a teacher, passing on knowledge and understanding in a chain without beginning or end. What we learn from our parents, we pass on to our children.

Shan, good.

Nothing is more important.

In this chapter, Lao Tzu stresses this basic duty shared by all. The teacher must teach all he or she knows, the student must be devoted to learning what is taught. Whatever reason they might have for neglecting this duty, they are mistaken.

Teaching is not the same as indoctrination. That would be intellectual molestation. True wisdom doesn't need force. It convinces by its own merit. Learning is no passive memorizing of the thoughts of others. It has to be done by active thinking, questioning, and coming to one's own conclusions.

But if nothing is taught, then there is no basis for conclusions, and if nothing is learned there is nothing to conclude.

Good Skills

When Lao Tzu begins with a list of what good skills accomplish, he explains what can be reached by proper teaching. What we learn in the process is far from useless. Although teaching might be done mainly in theory, the benefits are practical as well.

We excel if we pay attention to just about everything, and we progress from generation to generation by passing on our knowledge and our experiences.

Thereby, we follow the light of every new dawn, when

days follow one another in the same cyclic progression that generations do.

The good and bad used in this chapter are not necessarily moral judgments on character, like we mostly use the words in the Western tradition.

The Chinese word for good, *shan*, relates to skill, excellence, and being in accordance with nature, but also kindness. The expression for bad is simply a negation of good, *pu shan*, which is somebody lacking these qualities. No ill will is assumed.

So, teaching is to help the student gain what was lacking.

28

Knowing the manly, but clinging to the womanly,
You become the valley of the world.
Being the valley of the world,
Eternal virtue will never desert you,
And you become like a little child anew.

Knowing the bright, but clinging to the dark,
You become a model to the world.
Being a model to the world,
Eternal virtue will never falter in you,
And you return to the boundless.

Knowing honor, but clinging to disgrace,
You become the valley of the world.
Being the valley of the world,
Eternal virtue will be full in you,
And you return to the state of uncarved wood.

When the uncarved wood is split,
Its parts are put to use.
When the sage is put to use,
He becomes the head.
The best way to carve is not to split.

Be Like Uncarved Wood

Lao Tzu is fond of the image of the uncarved wood as a symbol of simplicity and humility. He uses it several times in his book. A piece of wood is as simple as something can ever be, but it contains numerous possibilities. When carved, it can become almost anything you want. Still, nothing surpasses the natural state of wood before the knife is put to it.

We should not think that we improve the wood by our carving. We just change it. That way it may become more useful to us, but in no way finer than it was in its original state.

This is even more obvious if compared to what it was when still part of a living tree, where it participated in the wonderfully complex process of life and growth. When cut from that tree it becomes a log. A chunk of material, passively reduced to whatever we make of it, or abandoned and decomposed.

Whatever we do to wood, it can never be as splendid as it was on the living tree.

Polarities

In this chapter, Lao Tzu also uses quite strong polarities, such as honor and disgrace, preferring the latter. That might be hard for most people to accept. But insisting on being honored is a mentality that surely leads to disgrace.

The one who accepts disgrace, on the other hand, will be honored already by this.

We frequently witness examples of this in modern day politics, where pompous dignitaries fall from grace when they refuse to admit any wrongdoings, although evident. Those who confess humbly and regretfully, on the other hand, can find themselves even more praised than ever before. We do love to forgive a repenting sinner.

Choosing the darkness before the bright seems even more absurd to us, because we have a tradition of comparing the latter to salvation and the former to its opposite, damnation. It's deeply rooted in the Christian vocabulary, since the time when Jesus called himself the light. Consequently, we call his counterpart the prince of darkness.

But the opposites mean something else to Lao Tzu. Darkness refers to the dim valley compared to the brightly lit mountain, the shady side, *yin*, instead of the sunny side *yang*. *Tao Te Ching* keeps repeating the ideal of yielding, so the sage modestly steps out of the light, into the shadows, and never insists on attention.

The Chinese words used can also be translated white and black, but the meaning is the same. Choosing the latter shows exemplary character, because it proves that you are not driven by personal gain.

The manly and womanly are opposites of the same kind as light and dark. Yang is regarded as manly and yin as womanly, in the Chinese tradition. In the symbol, yang is the white field hovering over the black yin, like Heaven rises above Earth.

Anyone choosing the former will elevate himself over others, thereby losing compassion for them. It's impossible to lift everyone else to an elevated position, but if you choose the lowest seat, then others will fall effortlessly into your lap.

Usually, Lao Tzu compares this yielding to the motherly, but here he lets us know that it also brings out the child in us.

When you let go of your ambitions, the world becomes fresh before your eyes. You see it for what it is, instead of what you want from it. That's the eye of the child.

Yin and yang. The signs show the original meaning of the words: shady side and sunny side.

The Virtuous Past

The virtue mentioned several times in this chapter is *Te*, part of the book's title. This virtue being eternal refers to its ancient tradition. It could not be eternal without stretching into the past as well as into the future.

In the time of Lao Tzu, the ancient past was regarded with much more reverence than the present and the future. So, that side of eternity was valued higher. Virtue of recent origin would be regarded as preposterous.

Antiquity, not only in China, valued its history tremendously, but saw little reason to ponder the future at any length. We tend to do the opposite, because we believe the future to be one of continued improvement – at least its potential.

If you make the right choices by following the ancient virtue, you become like a child, simple as uncarved wood, and thereby boundless. You lose the limits of preconception, the prejudice brought on by wants and ambitions.

It's a state of mind, which is brought on by virtuous choices – not for the sake of reaching it, but because of these choices being the virtuous ones. That's why virtue fills you, never falters, and never deserts you. True virtue needs neither reason nor rewards. It's just the way it should be, which is according to the Way.

Put to Use
Lao Tzu ends the chapter with what seems to be some play with words. The sage is like uncarved wood, which is put to use when split. But when the sage is put to use, he takes command. Some serve and some lead. It's natural for the sage to lead, even when he is reluctant to do so.

He will lead even when others expect him to serve. He points the Way. How else to use him?

The sage knows to remain in the state of uncarved wood, utter simplicity, in whatever grand tasks he gets involved. He is not split, either by distraction or ambition, but remains with what we call the whole picture.

That's how the world should be treated. It's a whole that must not be split into this and that. All things are connected to the whole, and malfunction when separated from it.

This is something we are right now starting to understand about the world we live in. We give this knowledge a fancy new name, ecology, but it's been known for ages.

29

Conquering the world and changing it,
I do not think it can succeed.
The world is a sacred vessel that cannot be changed.
He who changes it will destroy it.
He who seizes it will lose it.

So, among all things,
Some lead and some follow,
Some sigh and some pant,
Some are strong and some are weak,
Some overcome and some succumb.

Therefore the sage avoids extremity, excess, and extravagance.

Don't Change the World

Lao Tzu continues his ecological thinking, more than two millennia ahead of time. In his own era, he was not alone in appreciating the world as it was, but he expressed it with rare sharpness and devotion.

 He would not have approved of the Great Wall of China, which was begun around the time when this book is supposed to have been written. That colossal wall, which grew and grew by each century, is such a striking symbol of what Lao Tzu deplored, one must wonder if he watched its beginning with his own eyes.

 The emperors, who tried to hold onto their vast domain by enclosing it, were indeed headed towards the failure he foresaw.

The bigger things are, the more difficult they are to grab and keep. The world is simply too much. So are countries, even rather small ones. Any one of them has had countless rulers, even dynasties, where the mightiest of kings have been replaced, borders have been moved, treasures have changed owners, and castles have been vacated. Power is not persistent.

Many have tried to change the whole world or some significant parts of it. We seem to be getting good at it, lately. But each such change must be constantly renewed and fortified. Otherwise, the world will soon return to its previous state. Man-made changes wither, often quicker than men do.

Nature gnaws down unattended buildings, grass pierces through asphalt, and forests move in on lawns that aren't mowed regularly. Animals, too, feast on civilization as they do on nature. The changes we make are splendid only in our own eyes, and we should refrain from blinking if we want the sight to remain.

Change Is the Nature of Nature

What makes the world difficult to change in a lasting way is not its reluctance to change, but because it's so familiar with it. The world itself is a master of change. That's how it was made in the first place, and that's how it continues to remake itself.

From the smallest to the biggest part of the world, everything changes. Water evaporates, rising to the sky, and falls back on the ground as rain. Forests grow, burn down, and grow back up again. Even the vast continents move across the surface of the planet, as if playing their own Rubik's Cube.

Our whole planet is spinning around its axis, and

around the sun, in a remarkable race which is still insignificant compared to the movements of galaxies and the expansion of the whole universe. Everything is changing, and most of those changes are far superior to anything the human being can accomplish.

We don't fail because we try to change things, but because we want to stop them from changing. What little adjustments we do to the world, we don't want undone. We build our houses and want them to remain exactly as they were immediately after the roofing.

That's futile. Decay starts already at the beginning of growth. Change has neither beginning nor end. We can never fully control it, since we are mere parts of it.

So, what Lao Tzu states about the consequences would be true, if change and seizure of the world were at all possible. If the world could be changed into a fixed state, which is what we would try, it could only lead to destruction. We would have to stop time, and where would that leave us?

Costly Dreams

There is an order to life, and we play our parts in it. That's fine, and grants us enough liberty to explore our capacities and take delight in them. But if we try to overstep our boundaries, extend beyond our capacities, we will fail miserably and painfully.

There is no satisfaction in pretense, if allowed to guide our lives. We need to be what we are, not what we would like to be. Otherwise we can never come to like ourselves, and then we will never be pleased.

Lao Tzu understands the temptation of overdoing things and reaching beyond our wildest dreams. But he also knows about the price that needs to be paid for it. It's inevitable, since chasing our dreams means running away from our reality.

He wants us to start by reexamining what we have and what we are, because he is confident that doing so, we will find it to be sufficient. Then we can enjoy it. What more to ask for?

30

Those who advice the ruler on the Way,
Do not want the world subdued with weapons.
Such deeds bring on retaliation.
Thorn bushes grow where armies have camped.
Battles are followed by years of famine.
Therefore, good leaders reach solutions,
And then stop.
They do not dare to rely on force.

Solutions without arrogance,
Solutions without scorn,
Solutions without pride,
Solutions without benefit,
Solutions without domination.

Things exalted then decay.
This is going against the Way.
What goes against the Way meets an early end.

Peaceful Solutions

We are all aware that war is the worst. Still, there are not many years in history when the world has been free of wars. Are there any countries that have escaped them completely?

There have been recent claims that democratic nations have never been at war with one another. That might be true. It makes sense. The basic principle of democracy is that it's ruled by what the majority of the people want, and peace is certainly on the top of that list.

Democratically governed nations are therefore very unlikely to commence war.

Unfortunately, there are still plenty of nations governed differently, and there the statistics are less promising. Democracies have not avoided war, although they never initiated them. Other countries did. History, from ancient times to the present, tells us that we should not count on avoiding wars in the future.

Lao Tzu comes to the same sad conclusion. There will be wars. What he advices is to avoid them, and if they commence anyway, to swiftly end them. It's accomplished by remaining with that priority. Additional ambitions are only likely to prolong the war. Victory may even turn into defeat, if the troops are not halted or the peace is not fair.

Not victory, but a swift end to the war should be the goal. There is a difference. The warrior who hungers for victory will indulge in it and try to extend it. For each victory the hunger will increase, and each new enemy will be treated with less mercy.

The one who longs to lay down arms will not stoop to arrogance, scorn, pride, and the like. Even in the midst of battle, the wish for peace must be vivid.

War brings its own rhetoric. The enemy is said to be evil, so the war is just, no matter at what cost. Hatred arises in the pain and the fury, and it doesn't stop when the war does. The winners want to punish their former enemies, who become bitter and plot revenge.

That's not peace. Although the war might have been started by the ones defeated, peace is always primarily the responsibility of the winners. The way they handle it decides how long it will last.

This is no news to us. We have known it for as long as

we have had wars. Still, it's easily forgotten at the end of the next one. That may be one of the major causes for the persistent reappearance of war. Forgive and forget, we say, but we rarely do.

The last lines of this chapter give the impression of changing the subject, but the victorious are often exalted. That's the beginning of their downfall, which is accelerated if they encourage and participate in their own exaltation. We quickly get fed up with praising a winner who lacks modesty. Well, even the modest idols have a hard time keeping their fans for any length of time.

Heroes of a battle do wisely to escape, well before the celebration becomes tiresome to those participating in it.

31

Weapons are ominous tools.
They are abhorred by all creatures.
Anyone who follows the Way shuns them.

In peaceful times, the noble ruler honors the left side.
At war, he honors the right side.

Weapons are ominous tools.
They are not the noble ruler's tools.
He only uses them when he can't avoid it.
Peace and quiet are preferred.
Victory should not be praised.
Those who praise victory relish manslaughter.
Those who relish manslaughter
Cannot reach their goals in the world.

At times of joy, the left side is honored.
At times of grief, the right side is honored.
At battle, the second in command stands to the left,
And the commander in chief to the right.
This means they stand as in funerals.

When many people are killed
They should be mourned and lamented.
Those who are victorious in war
Should follow the rites of funerals.

Victory Is Cause for Grief

Lao Tzu continues his reflections on war, begun in the previous chapter. Again, he protests any tendency to glorify it. War should be entered reluctantly and in grief. This is true for both parties, whatever the outcome. The noble warrior mourns the fallen ones, also those of the enemy.

War erupts as a consequence of some serious failure. People will die, and the outcome can be expected to accomplish no more than a correction of the initial failure. Maybe not even that. War improves nothing and rarely solves any problem. It's a funeral of grotesque proportions. What else to do but grieve it?

Weapons are nothing but tools of war and should be regarded as such. It would be vicious to call them beautiful or praise their effectiveness. They may be needed in the defense against tools of the same kind. There is no other need for them and no other value to them.

Weapons are needed, sadly, because they exist.

Still, all through history – in China as well as in every other country – war and its tools have been glorified. They still are. We revel at skillfully crafted weapons, their sharpness and precision. We turn past wars into legends of heroism and triumph, as if man excels only in such challenges.

We make wars exciting and regard peace as little more than the dull time between them. Peace is described as non-war, as if lacking any value or significance of its own. We would do much better to regard war as non-peace, moments of meaningless interruption in the process of history.

War just kills, but peace is really what we live for. Strangely, we seem to forget that in times of peace. Why do we need wars to remind ourselves of the blessing of peace?

Lao Tzu points at a fundamental flaw in our attitude. We quickly forget the horrors of war when they are absent, because we confuse the joy we felt at their end with the triumph of victory. The celebration of the return of peace becomes a cheering of the soldiers who ended the war by winning it. When soldiers are praised, so is war, whatever the returning soldiers might think about it.

No, war must be regarded as a funeral all through. That's what it is.

32

The Way is ever nameless.
Though simple and subtle,
The world cannot lead it.
If princes and kings could follow it,
All things would by themselves abide,
Heaven and Earth would unite
And sweet dew would fall.
People would by themselves find harmony,
Without being commanded.

As soon as rules were made, names were given.
There are already many names.
One must know when it is enough.
Those who know when it is enough will not perish.

What the Way is to the world,
The stream is to the river and the sea.

All Follow Those Who Follow Tao

This chapter starts with a reminder of what was stated in the very first chapter of the *Tao Te Ching*: no name does justice to Tao, the Way. Lao Tzu has chosen the term Tao for the great mystery he discusses, but he hurries to add that a name is just a name, and not the thing named – not even an adequate description of it.

This might seem to be a warning of little significance,

but we have a tendency to name things and thereby start to pretend that we understand and control them.

A lot of our natural science is done like that. We observe a phenomenon, like the apple falling from the tree, and we name it gravity, pretending that thereby, it has become part of our knowledge of the world. Well, we have found mathematical circumstances under which gravity operates, but we still don't know what it is. The name doesn't explain it anymore than its manifestations do. We are still to find out what it really is.

That's true for many more of our scientific explorations than we would be comfortable to admit. Names are just names, descriptions are just descriptions. A true understanding of what's going on demands fundamental knowledge of how our universe operates, and why. That's still far off.

This is what Lao Tzu reminds us, with words that seem to contain a sigh. There are indeed already many names. It was true in his time and even more so in ours. We have so many names, but do we really understand much more about the world we live in?

We would spontaneously say yes, but then again we confuse true knowledge with putting names to phenomena we have observed and catalogued. Even though we have found plenty of mathematical relations between natural phenomena, it still doesn't prove we understand them.

We observe a lot, but we understand less.

That's why scientific theory is no more certain than to last until a better theory comes along. Along the way, we just have to do with what we've got, and hope that it will suffice for our applications of it.

We do quite well. We send rockets to the moon and beyond it. We build big steel vessels that fly a hundred times faster than the birds. We cure deadly diseases, but we also invent new ways of killing more effectively than they ever did. Our science allows us feats that our predecessors would call magic. But it doesn't mean we understand the universe and our place in it any more profoundly.

Lao Tzu calls for a humble search of what is the real essence, not just superficial manifestations of it. That call is just as relevant today as it was more than two thousand years ago.

Prime Mover

Albert Einstein dreamed about a united field theory in which all of the forces at play in the universe would be combined into one fundamental energy, explaining just about everything. We all have the same dream of finding the ultimate why, what Aristotle called the Prime Mover, a first cause in the world, something that started everything and therefore still holds the key to it all.

That's what Lao Tzu calls Tao, readily admitting that it's beyond his understanding, although he has a lot to say about how it operates.

Tao is Aristotle's Prime Mover, Einstein's united field theory, and the incentive of the creator god in the religions. We could also call it the condition igniting the Big Bang. So many names.

Lao Tzu is practical. Instead of struggling to understand what might lie far beyond our capacity, let's be perceptive to the patterns and follow the directions pointed out by how nature behaves. Even though the essence of Tao remains a mystery, we can follow its path. If we do, the world will treat us gently and all its creatures will prosper.

33

Those who understand others are clever,
Those who understand themselves are wise.
Those who defeat others are strong,
Those who defeat themselves are mighty.

Those who know when they have enough are rich.
Those who are unswerving have resolve.
Those who stay where they are will endure.
Those who die without being forgotten get longevity.

Longevity

The last line of this chapter has usually been understood as a hint to actual longevity, the possibility to escape death. It was interpreted as saying: "Those who die without perishing get longevity." This was also the Chinese understanding of the line.

But in the 1970's, two *Tao Te Ching* manuscripts were found in Mawangdui, dating back to around the year 200 BC. They were hundreds of years older than the previously known versions of the text. Both of these manuscripts have the wording I use above, making much more sense.

Lao Tzu has no faith in escaping death, but being remembered by one's fellow men is defeating it in a significant way.

The misunderstanding of this line influenced Chinese Taoists of old substantially. There were many of them believing that a Taoist life could lead to extreme longevity, even immortality, and they experimented with potions to accom-

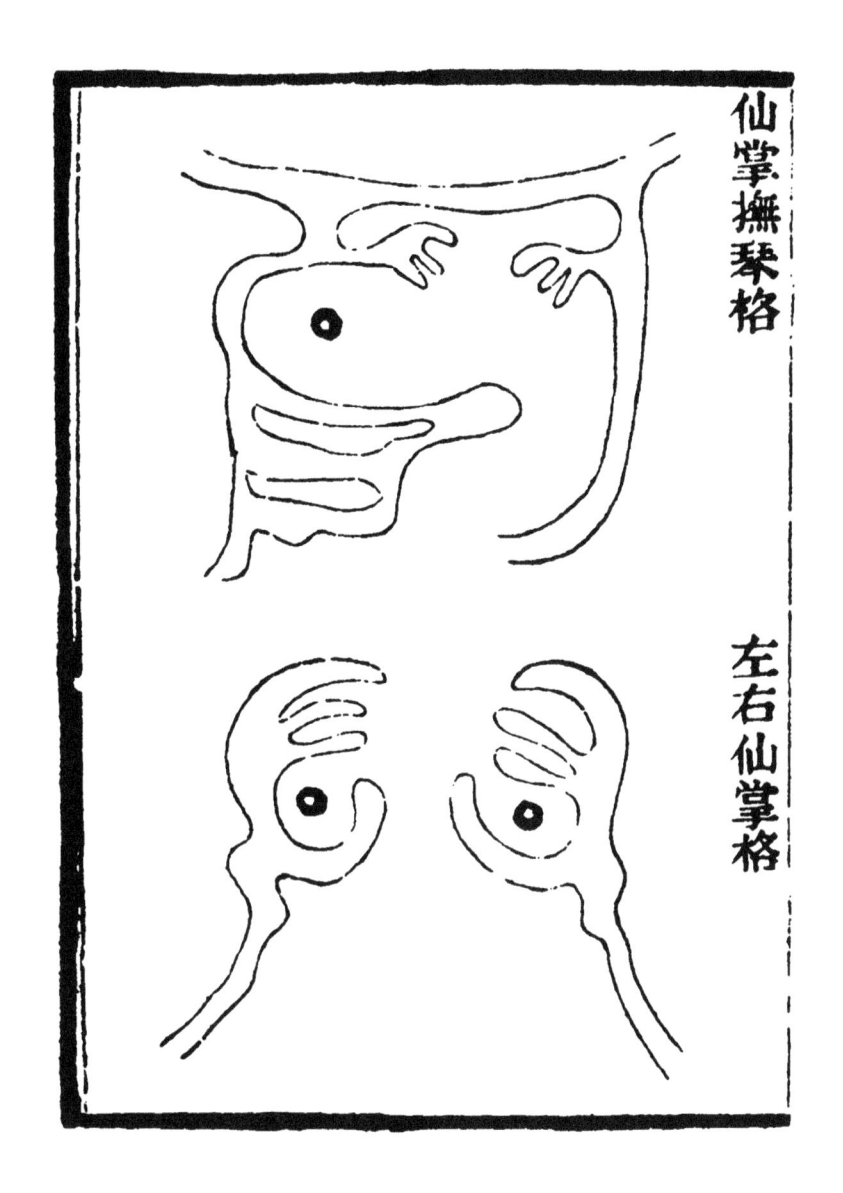

Above, the hands of an immortal playing the lute. Below, the hands of an immortal. Illustration from the 18th century. In religious Taoism, Tao Chiao, there was a belief in immortality. There were also elaborate methods for reaching it. Philosophical Taoism, Tao Chia, had no such illusion, nor did Lao Tzu.

道德經

plish it. Some of these potions contained poisonous heavy metals, so they reached eternal life quicker than expected.

Death is the monster that we have to fight in our minds, from childhood to old age. Coming to terms with it is probably the greatest of quests. Most religions have this dilemma at their core, presenting all kinds of solace.

Many myths of antiquity describe death and the afterlife with horror. This is true for the oldest book we know, *Gilgamesh*, and for the beliefs of the ancient Egyptians. Death was seen as a passage into a dreadful world that anyone would want to avoid at all cost.

So, the search for longevity was pursued in many cultures and in so many ways. We still search, with no less frenzy. We would be wiser to spend our energy on making the time we have meaningful.

Improving Life

If we learn to understand ourselves and improve by overcoming our personal limitations, then we have come a long way towards Lao Tzu's version of longevity. We will also benefit from halting our greed, holding on to our resolve, and doing the best of where we are, instead of hurrying elsewhere.

Lao Tzu keeps repeating that happiness is not to be found anywhere but here and now. Chasing it elsewhere is just fleeing the possibility of finding it.

That doesn't necessarily mean we should be content with whatever situation we are in. Change is sometimes needed, but we should begin by asking ourselves if that's really so, and to what the change we might plan will really lead.

Lao Tzu would probably be the first to point out that we

know what we have, but not what we might get. That's reason to be cautious.

Returning to the last line of the chapter, its message has been stated also by others, in other times and other places. *Havamal*, the Old Norse collection of proverbs, states it more bluntly: "Animals die, friends die, so will you. I know one thing that never dies – the judgment on a dead man."

34

The great Way is all-pervading.
It reaches to the left and to the right.
All things depend on it with their existence.
Still it demands no obedience.
It demands no honor for what it accomplishes.
It clothes and feeds all things without ruling them.

It is eternally without desire.
So, it can be called small.
All things return to it,
Although it does not make itself their ruler.
So, it can be called great.

Therefore, the sage does not strive to be great.
Thereby he can accomplish the great.

It's Great to Be Small

Lao Tzu again describes the humble nature of Tao, the Way. Its greatness lies exactly in its modesty. It has made the world appear and keeps it from disappearing. Every creature exists because of it. Yet, it's discreet with its presence, as if hiding, and it allows us to follow it or not, as if we had a choice to alter the very laws of existence.

The first cause of the universe is quiet about its feat.

This grand example is for everyone to follow. The sage, knowing this, makes sure not to strive for greatness. What would at all be great compared to Tao? One learns Tao by imitating it, so the sage avoids greatness – not in order to accomplish it, but to be in accordance with Tao, the greatest of all. This imitation leads to great accomplishments.

It can also be described as behaving in accordance with nature. When we learn the natural way, we find solutions to problems no matter how big they are, and our actions meet no resistance. We still have the freedom to counter nature, and often we succeed. The question is what it costs us. And we continue paying as long as we want to keep it up.

We can fly, although it's not within our own nature. It took quite an effort to succeed, and it continues to be a complicated endeavor. Lao Tzu would have preferred us to remain on the ground. We change the courses of rivers, drill tunnels through mountains, drain lakes, and tear down forests. It's not for free.

That's Our Nature
On the other hand, this refusal to accept nature's order is part of our nature. That's how we are, evidently. We developed this big brain and need to use it. So, we replace nature by culture. Cities expand and we hurry between them at increasing speed.

It may pillage our planet, but we can't stop ourselves. We are victims of our own capacity.

Lao Tzu was surely aware of this paradox. Already in his days, this urge of ours had forced nature to retreat a few steps. He could see civilization grow, and didn't expect his fellow men to reverse the process.

Instead of restraining our urge to excel, maybe the solution lies in developing how this urge is expressed. If the brain is what causes it, why not turn the ambitions to it?

Instead of struggling with our outer world in efforts to improve it, which is a quest that seems endless, we might find greater satisfaction by working on our inner worlds. Our minds. They are worlds just as complex as the one we see around us.

Exploring the mind, cultivating our thoughts, contemplating our awareness – that's where we are the most likely to find the answers to the questions with the same origin. That's also how to satisfy our longing, without ravaging the world around us.

It could also lead to the discovery that there is not so much we need from the outside world.

35

Hold on to the great image,
And the whole world follows,
Follows unharmed,
Content and completely at peace.

Music and food make the traveler halt.
But words spoken about the Way have no taste.
When looked at, there's not enough to see.
When listened to, there's not enough to hear.
When used, it is never exhausted.

Elusive, But Never Exhausted

The image that Lao Tzu refers to is Tao, the Way. The word he uses also means appearance, similarity, and likeness. One might call it an impression or a symbol. He wants to make clear that the elusive Tao is more than its image. What we see of it is much less than what it is.

Still, what we perceive is what we see and hear, so we need to go in the direction pointed out by our senses – yet, constantly reminding ourselves that there is more to it and that the Way reaches farther than we are able to detect. If we hold on to it and go where it leads, we will find that the whole world complies and benefits as well.

Although Tao is hard to see or hear, and words to describe it become far from spectacular, it's inexhaustible. That's because it's not a thing or a creature, but a principle, a natural law that governs the universe. Tao is the way the universe works. The whole universe may dissolve without

Hsiang, image, also meaning elephant.

the law of its fate doing so. Like a formula it can be used over and over and over, without suddenly ceasing to function.

This is more evident to us than to people of antiquity. They saw everything in the world as expressions of struggling powers, whether those were divinities or other forces. Therefore, they could imagine the sun one morning refusing to rise, or crops one year failing completely to grow. They had little idea of irresistible natural laws that Heaven and Earth and all things therein could but obey.

Nowadays, we imagine the universe completely controlled by nothing but natural laws, without any will of its own or any will beyond it. We regard it all as machinery. This image comes closer to Lao Tzu's idea of Tao, but it lacks some of the poetry and beauty of the latter.

Strangely, the word for image, *hsiang*, also means elephant. This probably stems from a time when elephants could only be seen on pictures from other parts of the world.

36

What should be shrunken must first be stretched.
What should be weakened must first be strengthened.
What should be abolished must first be cherished.
What should be deprived must first be enriched.

This is called understanding the hidden.
The soft and weak overcome the hard and strong.

The fish cannot leave the deep waters.
The state's weaponry should not be displayed.

One Postulates the Other

Ancient Chinese thought is often done in polarities, like yin and yang. They are not alone in that. In many traditions around the world, existence is seen as the dynamics between two opposites. They may be light and dark, high and low, hot and cold, life and death, good and bad, and so on. Lao Tzu is also fond of it, although he sees a single unity, Tao, at the very root of it all.

In this chapter he mentions examples of opposite directions or actions, instead of opposite fixed states. Stretching is one direction, shrinking is its opposite. What he claims about their relation implies mutual dependence, comparable to what happens in our breathing. We must inhale before we can exhale, and exhale before we can inhale. There is no ideal middle point, between exhalation and inhalation. If we remain there we suffocate.

The opposites are interacting continuously. It's never

just one or the other, not even a resting place between them. Things shrink or expand, they are weakened or strengthened, but never completely still. People are cherished or abolished, enriched or deprived, but never stay for long in one solid state of affairs. The whole universe is all about movement and change.

Not even in death is stillness achieved. What dies will start to decay and decompose, later to reappear as material in a new creature. We may die, but we don't stop moving. That's the kind of immortality we know for certain. Nothing ever halts.

Considering this, we can look at the processes Lao Tzu mentions, and other similar examples, with different eyes. If we are to accept how Tao makes the world progress, we should not seek for balance between opposites. We should adapt to the revolving changes, since they are unavoidable. Whatever stops changing ceases to exist, if that's at all possible.

When we are cherished we should be aware that the opposite is near at hand. The more you are praised above others, the higher the risk that they get tired of it and turn their backs to you.

People even allow themselves to do that for puny reasons, because they have praised the person previously, as if that is an excuse. The less you are elevated, the less your fall will be.

There will be moments when we are elevated, be it minutely, and moments when we fall from that height. We should avoid getting carried away by the former or getting desperate when the latter occurs. We can't expect to escape it completely in life.

The same goes for being enriched and deprived. The

more we get, the more we risk losing. Certainly, nobody goes through life without ever getting or losing something, so again we just have to treat these occurrences with the appropriate calm.

If we don't strive for the highest seats or the greatest riches, but relax and remind ourselves that few things last, then the turns of fate have less effect on us. We soften, so we don't break, and we weaken, so we don't fight too hard against events that unfold.

It might seem like surrendering, and somehow it is, but most things we can give up without actually losing much. One should choose one's battles carefully.

Hide the Weapons

Battle leads us to the last lines of the chapter, with the advice to hide the state's weaponry, like the fish hides deep in the sea.

It seems out of place in this chapter, and it might very well be. As mentioned before, the 81 chapters of the *Tao Te Ching* are a later division. The original text had no such thing. There were period marks here and there, through the text, but no chapters. When this division was made, inevitably some lines were grouped in ways that Lao Tzu didn't intend.

This may be one such example. The two bottom lines, about fish and weaponry, make a perfectly reasonable whole.

Any experienced soldier would agree that it's good strategy not to flaunt one's weapons and all one's military power. What is unknown raises more fear than even the largest army does. Unseen weapons are more threatening to the enemy than the sharpest and shiniest swords.

Also, who is sure of having military superiority? The enemy, too, might hide some of his forces, maybe even most of them.

When you can count your enemies, you dare to confront them. You are much more reluctant to do so when their numbers are unknown.

In European history it was common to regard the number of the population as a state secret, especially in countries where they assumed that neighboring countries were more populated – or when they had learned that their own numbers were overestimated by the neighbors.

All through history, the militaries have been quite secretive, for this or other reasons. The less the enemy knows, the better.

There is a personal side to this strategy. The cherished and enriched should avoid displaying this, or they might invite a forced change to the opposite. If they are hard and strong, they should for the same reason try to present themselves as soft and weak. Nobody is mighty enough to afford provoking those who surround him.

37

The Way is ever without action,
Yet nothing is left undone.
If princes and kings can abide by this,
All things will form themselves.
If they form themselves and desires arise,
I subdue them with nameless simplicity.
Nameless simplicity will indeed free them from desires.

Without desire there is stillness,
And the world settles by itself.

Nameless Simplicity

Tao Te Ching is traditionally divided into two parts. One is called Tao, the Way, simply because its first chapter begins with that word, and the other is called Te, virtue, because that's the word its first chapter begins with. This, the 37th chapter of the book, is the last of the first part.

In the two manuscripts found in Mawangdui, dating to around the year 200 BC, the two parts have the opposite order. There, the whole book ends with this chapter – quite suitably with the words about the stillness in which the world settles by itself.

In spite of the Mawangdui manuscripts, I present the book in its traditionally established order. Otherwise it would get complicated for the reader to compare different versions of the text. Also, it's the path taken by most experts on this classic.

Myself, I find that the first chapter defining Tao, and the

P'u, uncarved wood, simplicity.

last one stating the purpose of the noble man's Tao, make perfect sense as the beginning and the end of the book. So, in spite of the Mawangdui manuscripts, I am inclined to trust the traditional order of the chapters more.

Simplicity

As for the word 'simplicity' used in this chapter, its pictogram is the one for the uncarved wood, which is an image of utter simplicity that Lao Tzu favors in the book. He has used it several times before this chapter.

This image presents simplicity as a rough and unrefined state of affairs, a natural form before altered by cultural or other ambitions. Things as they are before human intervention.

When Lao Tzu also calls it nameless, he hints on its close relation to Tao, the Way, since namelessness is one of its traits. This was pointed out already in the first chapter, which states that the way that can be walked is not the real Way, and the name that can be named is not the real name of it.

The uncarved wood lacking a name is similar to Tao, in the sense of being beyond description. The simplicity that can free all things of desire is not just any simplicity, but that of Tao, the simple truth behind all.

Tao needs not act, since its law decides how everything

Yu, desire.

else has to act. If rulers abide, they follow the same law instead of fighting it. Then things will happen by themselves and the turn of events will be natural, according to the terms of the universe. Things move on as they should.

Desire

The word desire is used in 15 of the 81 chapters of the *Tao Te Ching* (chapters 1, 3, 15, 19, 29, 34, 36, 37, 39, 46, 57, 61, 64, 66, 77). The Chinese word, *yu*, isn't directed just at sexual desires, but at any kinds of longings, wants, lusts, and wishes.

Lao Tzu doesn't really ban it, but he is clear about the benefit of being free of it. Desire is part of the human character, and therefore hard to avoid. There is no point in trying to suppress it completely, but those who follow Tao will find a way to make it dissolve.

In the sage, it no longer decides what action to take.

Desire is what risks interfering with the natural process, this chapter tells us. Greed is a kind of desire. So is hunger for power, and that for making a mark in history. When people interfere with the natural chain of events, they want to change them into more personally profitable outcomes. That disturbs the order of all. It has no chance of succeeding, but it can cause a lot of damage before failing.

Personal desire is as easy to understand as it is likely to

appear, especially with people who have the power to make them imagine that they can fulfill it. We all want to make the most of our lives. If that means countering the natural cause of things, then we will make a lot of noise, cause a lot of trouble, but at the end we will find that we accomplished nothing durable.

We do better to accept things as they are, and find our place inside these patterns. There is a good place to be found for everyone, without upsetting the harmony. Actually, only by joining with the harmony are we ever likely to find that place.

Te

德

Virtue

上德不德是以有德
下德不失德是以無德
上德無為而無以為
下德無為而有以為
上仁為之而無以為
上義為之而有以為
上禮為之而莫之以應
則攘臂而扔之
故失道而後德
失德而後仁
失仁而後義
失義而後禮
夫禮者忠信之薄而亂之首
前識者
道之華而愚之始
是以大丈夫
處其厚　不居其薄
處其實　不居其華
故去彼取此

Chapter 38 of Tao Te Ching in Chinese. The Wang Pi version. The sign Te on the previous page is a calligraphy by the author.

38

The highest virtue is not virtuous.
Therefore it has virtue.
The lowest virtue holds on to virtue.
Therefore it has no virtue.

The highest virtue does nothing.
Yet, nothing needs to be done.
The lowest virtue does everything.
Yet, much remains to be done.

The highest benevolence acts without purpose.
The highest righteousness acts with purpose.
The highest ritual acts, but since no one cares,
It raises its arms and uses force.

Therefore, when the Way is lost there is virtue.
When virtue is lost there is benevolence.
When benevolence is lost there is righteousness.
When righteousness is lost there are rituals.
Rituals are the end of fidelity and honesty,
And the beginning of confusion.

Knowing the future is the flower of the Way,
And the beginning of folly.
Therefore,
The truly great ones rely on substance,
And not on surface,
Hold on to the fruit,
And not to the flower.
They reject the latter and receive the former.

道德經

The Highest Virtue

Here the focus is not on Tao, the Way, but on the second best: *Te,* virtue. Lao Tzu makes it very clear that virtue, although seemingly splendid, is what to follow in the absence of contact with Tao. This is true even for the very highest virtue. It's a symptom of deviation from the Way.

In our Western understanding, virtue is an old Latin concept with its roots in Ancient Greek and Roman thought. That's surely not what Lao Tzu considered in his choice of the Chinese word *te*. We have to examine carefully what the Chinese word might have meant to him, so that we don't automatically assume similarities with the Western concept.

But upon examination, the Chinese and the Latin words are not that far apart at all. The pictogram for *te* is a complex one, consisting of 14 brush strokes, which is a lot. It has three parts, each with its own separate meaning when not combined: to walk, to look straight forward, and the heart. To follow the heart in a straight walk forward.

We would think of walking the narrow road, as in Matthew 7: "The way is narrow that leads to life, and there are few who find it."

It's also quite interesting that the word Lao Tzu uses for what to do when the Way is lost, also contains the concept of walking. We have to walk through life, all of us who are born into it. How to find the correct direction? Virtue is to follow one's heart, and not deviate from this conviction.

But then we have a new problem of linguistics. Is the heart the same to the Chinese as it is to us?

In Western tradition, the word is rarely used just to point out that muscle pumping the blood around in the body. We have given the word connotations relating to emotions,

徳 *Te, virtue.*

ethics, conviction, and personal commitment. The Chinese have done something similar. The word is used for mind, intelligence, soul, stamina, character, and such things. Not that far from the Western use.

In short, to follow one's heart is equally commendable to the Chinese as it is to us.

For the above reasons, I dare to conclude that the Chinese word *te* is surprisingly near to our idea of virtue. So, virtue can be used rather safely in the translation of the *Tao Te Ching*. That's also the case in most translations of the book.

Virtue as a Substitute

Lao Tzu makes sense when speaking about virtue as an inferior thing to Tao itself. When we lose track, when the proper order of the universe is not evident to us, we have to trust our virtue, our sense of proper conduct. It's certainly not as safe as seeing the Way ahead of us.

We get lost repeatedly, because we are easily convinced of ideals that seem right at the time, but lead us astray. We listen to words, although Lao Tzu has warned us of their shortcomings. We use a lot of words.

Holding on to virtue is to trust it more than the Way itself, when it's revealed to us. Virtue is a poor replacement for the real thing, but it can be very seductive. So, many of us hurry to decide what's virtuous and what's not, and then take pride in holding on to their course without ever questioning it. Tragedy is a very likely result, as history has shown us again and again.

When we are convinced of being virtuous, we easily lose compassion as well as common sense. It's better to regard virtue with caution, so that we immediately discover when it leads to intolerance, prejudice, cruelty, and other deviations from Tao.

Tao is infinitely yielding, but virtue tends to be quite the opposite, when we hold on to it without any questioning.

Four Steps Down

Lao Tzu presents a descent in four steps from Tao. If Tao is lost, we only have virtue to guide our steps. If virtue is lost, we should try to behave benevolently, thereby causing the least damage possible in our confusion.

Benevolence needs no reason, since it acts from our hearts, our compassionate instincts. We want to do good, for no other reason than that good is superior to bad. We might not always know to separate the one from the other, but what we perceive as good we do without any other purpose.

If benevolence is lost, we turn to righteousness, but without benevolence and virtue it becomes a very risky business. Such righteousness can quickly lead to oppression and inhuman laws.

Righteousness always contains some purpose. We do this to accomplish that. The end justifies the means, although whenever this argument is put into use, it tends to lead to sacrifices surpassing the benefits of the outcome.

When even righteousness is lost, what remain are rituals – the ignorant commitment to customs and beliefs that have lost their meaning. That is mankind at its lowest, repeating things of old just because of habit, sticking desperately to outdated fragments of thoughts, as if their lack of reason were proof of their elevation. As if ignorance is bliss.

When rituals rule, force is always used to uphold them. They are not to be questioned, because there is no explanation to them. Unfortunately, it happens frequently that our society degrades to such practice.

The Folly of the Future
Lao Tzu ends the chapter with a warning about the future. Knowing it can be a splendid manifestation of the knowledge of Tao. When you are familiar with the Way, you know where it leads. But this is superficial. It's not where it leads that's important, but how the voyage is, at each small step of the Way. The present is what truly counts.

The future is just another word for the outcome, which is the excuse used by righteousness, as mentioned above. If we focus on what will happen later, we allow ourselves to mess up the present. Even if our view of the future is accurate, we have no reason for staring at it. It will come, in due time.

We do much better to keep our attention on the present. That's also the safest method to ensure that we reach the future we seek.

Tao is not about the future, although it rules that, too. It's about how everything works and should work at every moment of time. To follow its fruit instead of its dazzling flower is to adapt to Tao now, not at some other time.

39

These things of old obtained unity with the one.
Heaven obtained unity and became clear.
Earth obtained unity and became firm.
The spirits obtained unity and became deities.
The valleys obtained unity and became abundant.
All things obtained unity and became animate.
Princes and kings obtained unity and became rulers of the world.
They all obtained unity with the one.

If Heaven were not clear it might rend.
If Earth were not firm it might crumble.
If the spirits were not deities they might wither.
If the valleys were not abundant they might dry up.
If all things were not animate they might perish.
If princes and kings were not exalted they might be overthrown.

Therefore:
The noble must make humility his root.
The high must make the low its base.
That is why princes and kings call themselves orphaned, desolate, unworthy.
Is that not to make humility their root?

The separate parts make no carriage.
So, do not strive for the shine of jade,
But clatter like stone.

Unity with the One

The one is surely Tao, the Way. By conforming to Tao so much that it became unity, the powers of the world were established. Without that unity, they would lose their roots, and their substance would dissolve. This is no greater mystery to Lao Tzu, than it is to us that neither galaxies nor their stars and planets would have appeared without gravity to pull them together.

The expression 'all things' is literally 'the ten thousand things,' an old Chinese expression meaning so many things that it has to be all of them. Animals and people are also included, but as can be seen above, some significant powers or entities are not.

Spirits

One of these singled out entities is the spirit world. Some translations call them gods, but that says more about them than Lao Tzu is confirmed to have intended. What a god is differs from one tradition to another. The writer of the *Tao Te Ching* only mentions the divine a couple of times, in passing, as if not at all convinced of their existence. He certainly doesn't give them a significant role in the universe he describes.

The spirits he mentions might be ancestral souls. That's a common belief in many cultures of old. They might also be expressions of some animistic concept, regarding all things in nature as equipped with some kind of soul, life, or will. Whatever the case, they are not to be understood as spirits within living creatures, and Lao Tzu grants them no ruling role in his cosmos.

The line about the spirits becoming deities is difficult to

translate from the Chinese. The words used for spirit, *shen*, and deity, *ling*, are different, but almost synonymous. One might as well read the line as deities getting spirits – or even better: spirits getting souls.

Of course, all these three concepts are vague and completely dependent on to what culture they refer. Exactly what Lao Tzu might mean with the words he uses for them is not possible to deduct with any certainty. Fortunately, it's not necessary, since he gives them minimal importance.

In chapter 60, Lao Tzu mentions the ghosts, *kuei*, which are not identical to the deified spirits mentioned here, but the ghosts of deceased ancestors.

This chapter focuses on the necessity for the main parts of the world to be in accordance with Tao, or they will cease to function and there will be disorder. That goes for all the parts. They are equally needed in the grand scheme of things. So, there is no point in any one of them being exalted above the others. It's a team work, one might say, a great harmony where every piece fits, and nothing could be removed without damage to the whole.

That's reason for modesty. Humility is also the trait of Tao. Therefore, it would be hard to stay united without equal humility.

40

Returning is the movement of the Way.
Yielding is the manner of the Way.

All things in the world are born out of being.
Being is born out of non-being.

A Cyclic Universe

The returning movement of Tao, the Way, is cyclic. Tao brings everything forward, and then back to its origin, to be brought forward yet again. This is the view on nature shared by most cultures, and for obvious reasons.

Most of what takes place in nature is cyclic. Day and night take turns, the moon's phases are just as regular, as are the shifts of seasons through the year. Plants grow and then they wither. Animals have their lifespan, but also their offspring. That's the rhythm of mankind, too. Everywhere there is procreation, maybe including the universe as a whole.

What to make of it, but a cyclic principle ruling existence?

Although Tao is the instigator and instrument behind all these cycles, it accomplishes everything in the background, so that its role is hardly revealed. When we say that things happen of themselves, we unknowingly point out the work of Tao. The processes are carried out without apparent force. Things appear and disappear, move in their courses, and at no time do they show signs of being restricted or redirected.

It's as if Tao makes it all happen by opening doors instead of closing them, by making way instead of showing the way. That's also the superior ideal for any leader. They should use encouragement instead of threats, and opportunity instead of constraint. Nobody is pleased with constantly seeing the back of another, blocking the view ahead. The leader who is not opposed is the one showing the way by stepping out of it.

Being and non-being, *yu* and *wu*, are old concepts in Chinese thought, as well as in philosophy around the world. Some things deteriorate and disappear, as if they exist no more. Is that possible? Can something become nothing? Many philosophers have pondered the question. And vice-versa: can something appear out of nothing? Lao Tzu clearly states so, but other thinkers in history have doubted it.

In our time we have similar questions. Scientists seem to agree that the basic component of the universe, its energy, can change but not disappear – or appear out of nowhere.

On the other hand, the Big Bang theory implies that somehow, something must have come into existence, for the process to begin. Otherwise, that was not the moment when the universe was born. And what can we say about the domain that the universe has not yet reached in its expansion? It's said not to exist, since the universe is the limit for existence. But then the universe is something appearing out of nothing.

We still wrestle with the questions that Lao Tzu and many other ancient thinkers asked themselves.

41

The superior student listens to the Way
And follows it closely.
The average student listens to the Way
And follows some and some not.
The lesser student listens to the Way
And laughs out loud.
If there were no laughter it would not be the Way.

So, it has been said:
The light of the Way seems dim.
The progress of the Way seems retreating.
The straightness of the Way seems curved.
The highest virtue seems as low as a valley.
The purest white seems stained.
The grandest virtue seems deficient.
The sturdiest virtue seems fragile.
The most fundamental seems fickle.
The perfect square lacks corners.
The greatest vessel takes long to complete.
The highest tone is hard to hear.
The great image lacks shape.

The Way is hidden and nameless.
Still only the Way nourishes and completes.

Laughing Out Loud

What Lao Tzu says about students is true for all mankind. Some listen and learn, others do it sporadically, and those with the least respect just laugh and call it absurd. If there were no people reacting like that, it would probably not be Tao, the Way. Tao is absurd to the thoughtless mind.

Certainly, not only Tao meets this response in minds unwilling to ponder. Almost every breakthrough in science has met the same reaction – not just among the unknowing public, but also from several fellow scientists. Revelations are easily ridiculed by those who didn't come up with them.

It happened a lot to Charles Darwin, when he presented his theories about the evolution of the species. There were lots of caricatures in which he was portrayed as an ape, since people misunderstood him as saying that we evolved from them.

What he did say, of course, was that we as well as the other apes have evolved from common ancestors. But loads of people, even many who regarded themselves as both learned and reasonable, were outraged at the idea.

When Albert Einstein presented his idea that time is not a constant, but has a speed depending on the speed of the object on which it is measured, there were few who could grasp it. Many scientists doubted it for years, until measurements could be made that supported his theory. He got his Nobel Prize for something else, because his theory of relativity was still in dispute.

Actually, when we examine the history of science we notice that almost all significant breakthroughs have met with resistance and ridicule.

The reception of Tao among Lao Tzu's contemporaries had little chance of being any different. Mankind is reluctant to accept change, whether that change is one of thought or one of material circumstances.

What We Expect

We look at the world with prejudice, because we don't see what is, but what we want and expect. Tao in its yielding humility seems dim, whereas we expect great truth to shine like gold. Its progress seems retreating, because it makes little noise and shuns the spectacular. Its course seems curved and twisted, because it accomplishes its goals indirectly and discreetly.

Virtue is perceived similarly. Its highest form is the most humble, wherefore it seems as low as if cherished only by failing people. That's also why its grandest perspectives seem lacking, and its firmest rules seem faltering. We tend to expect the supreme to have the most impressive features, so we doubt any truth that lacks magnificence.

We expect grandeur, but the Way leads to the infinitesimal. That's where the secrets of the universe hide, as is currently confirmed by the science of quantum physics, not to mention string theory. The world is so grand, we go to telescopes to explore it, but its essence is ever-present and should rather be searched in microscopes.

42

The Way gave birth to one.
One gave birth to two.
Two gave birth to three.
Three gave birth to all things.

All things carry yin and embrace yang.
They reach harmony by blending with the vital breath.

What people loathe the most
Is to be orphaned, desolate, unworthy.
But this is what princes and kings call themselves.
Sometimes gain comes from losing,
And sometimes loss comes from gaining.

What others have taught, I also teach:
The forceful and violent will not die from natural causes.
This will be my chief doctrine.

Violence Meets a Violent End

This chapter consists of two parts, which have so little to do with one another that they were surely not originally intended to be combined. The first part deals with the creation of the world, and the second with commendable attitudes in human life.

There have been many theories about what Lao Tzu might mean with the one, two, three, in the first few lines. One should normally be Tao, the Way. So, did it give birth to itself? Well, it sort of did, since it has no other creator. Tao emerged, which is a kind of birth, and ignited the creation of the whole world.

The two would normally be yin and yang, the classical Chinese duo behind all polarities in the world – such as light and dark, high and low, male and female, and so on. Lao Tzu has stated earlier that he regards the emergence of yin and yang as belonging to the creation of the world. So, this may very well be what he implies here.

What three were born out of the two is much more difficult to ascertain. Heaven and Earth would have appeared early in any creation story of ancient China, as well as in most other cultures, but what might the third be?

Some say man, others say *ch'i* (also spelled *qi*), the vital breath. Man is more likely to be included among all things, appearing later, so the vital breath would be more likely here. The lines that follow do indeed support an early appearance of the vital breath.

Maybe the line should be read: "Two gave birth to the third." The Chinese wording of the text allows for this reading. It would need to mean that ch'i emerged out of yin and yang. This is actually similar to the Chinese tradition on the matter.

Still, I'm not convinced that Lao Tzu intended for these lines to be interpreted that literally. Maybe he was only suggesting that as soon as Tao broke up the original unity, which might be called chaos, then things started to appear, one after the other, in no particular order. Soon, there were ten thousand things, the Chinese expression for all things. He found no need to specify the exact order of appearance.

What he says about the behavior of all things is much more significant and precise. They carry yin and embrace yang. This is an elemental yin and yang principle. Both ex-

Yin and yang, the traditional Chinese polarity. Yin is the dark field and yang the light one above it. The dots represent the idea that there is always some yin in yang, and vice-versa. The symbol combining the two is also called T'ai Chi, the Supreme Origin. Ink painting by the author.

ist in everything, although sometimes in unbalanced proportions. Earth is the very signature of yin, and the same goes for Heaven and yang. Everything in between the two should be mixtures of yin and yang.

All things then reach harmony by blending with the vital breath, the life energy *ch'i*. Without it they would not remain and not have the ability to move or change. They would not be alive. About the vital breath, see chapter 10. It's also mentioned in chapter 55.

Orphaned, Desolate, and Unworthy
The second part of the chapter repeats what has been stated in chapter 39, about being orphaned, desolate, and unworthy. Here, Lao Tzu adds that gain can lead to loss, and loss to gain. This is an important warning. If rulers belittle themselves, their reputation gains from it. If they were to do the opposite, they would surely lose their reputation, eventually.

Still today, it's easy to reveal bad leaders, because they are almost always the ones most eager to be praised. That simply means they strive for personal gain. Usually, they don't seek just fame, but also fortune, increased power, and on and on.

The paradox of gain leading to loss is not only true for ruling, but for any endeavor. Aiming too high is bound to cause failure. Greed is costly, pride is shameful. In business, you can't get profit without investment. Personal relations don't last without compromise. Life is diluted if you only struggle to prolong it.

Moderation in all things is the most likely to succeed.

Violence

The last lines could very well be intended as separate from the preceding ones. It's a simple statement. Those who live violently risk dying the same way. History has shown us countless examples of it.

Here, too, moderation is to recommend. Lao Tzu repeats that we should avoid any extremes. Although he rarely makes moral judgments on people's life choices, he does confess that he is repelled by brutality, and by the search for personal gain gone wild.

He will come back to it in other chapters, but already here he is quite clear about it. Don't rock the boat, especially not for personal gain. Nature is rich enough to support us all in abundance, if there are not some who forcefully claim much more than their share.

Still, that's far from unknown to us.

43

The softest in the world
Surpasses the hardest in the world.
What has no substance
Can penetrate what has no opening.

Thereby I know the value of non-action.

The value of teaching without words
And accomplishing without action
Is understood by few in the world.

Non-Action

The principle of non-action, *wu-wei*, is frequently propagated in the *Tao Te Ching*. Often, the best solution is not to act at all, and when action is needed, to do as little as possible. Most things in the world correct themselves, given time. When impatience makes us hurry to solve them, we may make things worse.

The passivity Lao Tzu speaks of is no surrender, but the patience to wait for the outcome. One should show trust in Tao, the Way, and how it governs the universe towards harmony. In many cases, what we perceive as problems demanding our attention are merely phases on the way to a good outcome, in no need of our meddling. How can we be sure of contributing, when we don't even know what will happen by itself?

Certainly, there can be situations when we do need to take action, and quickly, for example to save lives or to avoid disaster. Lao Tzu doesn't deny it, but he doubts that such occasions should excuse our interference when not necessary or called for.

We human beings have a tendency to regard ourselves as motors of the world, as if nothing would happen – at least nothing good – without our initiative. It's a kind of *hubris* of our species. The other creatures on the planet do what is in their nature, fulfilling their natural needs, and leave it at that. We repeatedly take on the roles of the gods we believe in, imagining that we can do their job or correct it. That's not likely to end well.

As for words, when we express in words what should be taught from one generation to the next, we might be like the priest imploring his congregation to live as he speaks, not as he lives. Words are necessary when action is flawed. We teach what our own behavior doesn't display. If we could act correctly, we would not need words to transmit it.

Because we act incorrectly, and far too much, we need words to convey what we should have done or refrained from doing.

That which is the softest in the world is Tao, and it surpasses everything, no matter how hard. Also that, which has no substance and therefore penetrates all things, is Tao. Tao is everywhere, and behind everything, since before the dawn of time and beyond its final hour.

Those who follow Tao live in accordance with the world, so they make sure to be soft. In addition, although they are unable to lose substance, they put little value to it. They know that what is truly important is what seems not to exist at all.

44

Your name or your body,
What is dearer?
Your body or your wealth,
What is worthier?
Gain or loss,
What is worse?

Greed is costly.
Assembled fortunes are lost.
Those who are content suffer no disgrace.
Those who know when to halt are unharmed.
They last long.

Life Is the Treasure

What we know of is this life we are born into. Everything else is uncertain. So, why do we risk it by filling it with things that we don't really need? The only real treasure is life itself. Nothing else can possibly compare to it, much less surpass it.

But we easily forget that, when pursuing one or other superficial happiness.

True, it has merit to value one's name enough to make sure that others do it, too. With our words and deeds we decide how others will value us. Lao Tzu would add that our silence and the things we refrain from doing will influence our reputation even more.

On the other hand, when we make it our quest to reach fame and to receive praise that far exceeds what others get, then we put ourselves at risk, and forget that our names can never be more precious than our lives.

It's even more absurd when we devote our lives to assembling riches. When struggling to gather and keep a fortune, where's the time to enjoy it? You can't take it with you when you die. So, you risk spending your life chasing a longing that is never satisfied. Anybody pursuing that path is a victim of the fact that with wealth, there is never enough.

So, when you gain you are not pleased, and when you lose you are not pleased. Where's the pleasure? Greed is costly on one's peace of mind, and there is no reward for it. If you get rich enough, your name may be known and uttered with respect, even for generations to come. But your own life is pawned.

Enough is enough, and that's surprisingly little. When we are aware of this, we are practically invulnerable. This we can only be if we learn to value the fundamental asset we are given by living. Even in meager circumstances, our opportunities for great experiences and a truly rich life are as good as limitless.

45

The most complete seems lacking.
Yet in use it is not exhausted.
The most abundant seems empty.
Yet in use it is not drained.

The most straight seems curved.
The most able seems clumsy.
The most eloquent seems to stutter.

Movement overcomes cold.
Stillness overcomes heat.
Peace and quiet govern the world.

Appearances

Things aren't what they seem. We should not trust our perception, because it's rooted in our own mind's preconceptions. We often only see what we want to see, or what we expect to see. That may make life seem more agreeable to us, but it certainly flaws our judgment. Therefore, our actions easily go astray.

What is complete is whole, whereas we have a tendency to break things apart in order to find a quantity that overwhelms us. The whole is just one. We want many, and we don't see how anything less can be sufficient. But when parts are separated from the whole, they stop to function and deteriorate. Only the complexity of the whole is enough for all and forever.

Vast abundance is not perceivable, so we experience it as

diluted and desolate. What is everywhere is invisible to us, like the air around us. Our perception is focused on anomalies, on things that deviate from the mean.

That might be practical for our survival, but it also confuses our understanding of the world. We tend to make exceptions the rule, and miss the fundamental order of things.

The Fragile Environment

Also, sadly, we underestimate the importance of the fundamental components of our world. It took us far too long to realize our dependence on the environment we live in, because we have taken it for granted.

Lao Tzu's philosophy is firmly environmentalist, although his text precedes the invention of the word with more than two thousand years. He urges mankind to avoid interfering with the natural processes, or we do harm to them.

That's because we don't observe their importance, since we can't see their greatness. We cease to be aware of what we take for granted.

So, we have thoughtlessly polluted the very air that we breathe, because we can't see it. We also poison the water that we drink and the soil on which we grow what we eat. We treat our whole world as if it's dispensable.

Only now, on the verge collapse, have we been forced to realize the delicacy and importance of balance.

Skill

As for human perfection, we find it so rarely that we don't know what to make of it.

Those who really choose their words with care seem hesitant, even unsure. Something very similar is seen with those who really master some craft. They go about it with a calm that can be mistaken for incompetence, but the result is flawless and it's accomplished with amazing swiftness.

Refined movements look slow, because we perceive them clearly. The one who seems to move the slowest in a race is often the winner of it. When the foremost athletes excel in their sports, it looks so easy that we imagine we can do the same. That's the sign of perfection.

Balance

When Lao Tzu points out that movement overcomes cold and stillness overcomes heat, he points out the importance of balance. We know it to be quite true. Movement raises the temperature, and stillness decreases it. When we are cold we should get going and when we are hot we should calm down.

That is also true for situations where the temperature is symbolic. In a heated argument, silence is called for. When relations get chilled and indifference grows, we should spring into action.

The world benefits the most from peace and quiet, a state of balance and harmony. We can contribute to this if we remain sensitive to what is needed, and what is not.

46

When the Way governs the world,
The proud stallions drag dung carriages.
When the Way is lost to the world,
War horses are bred outside the city.

There is no greater crime than desire.
There is no greater disaster than discontent.
There is no greater misfortune than greed.

Therefore:
To have enough of enough is always enough.

Enough Is Enough

We learned in the previous chapter that peace should govern the world. That's what Tao, the Way, leads to when followed. When we deviate from the Way, war is imminent. By preparing for it, we guarantee that it will arrive. It would be nice with a world where war is not expected.

The following lines may well be regarded as a separate chapter. Their connection to the previous ones is indirect, to say the least. Not completely so, since war is often caused by desire, discontent, and greed. But war is not all they cause, although that must be the worst.

Desire may not be a crime in itself, but it often leads to one. Not only the crime of passion, which is more common than we ever care to admit. What we lust for is so difficult to resist that we allow ourselves criminal acts to get it, when our longing exceeds our restrain.

Discontent and greed are really expressions of desire. We are discontent when we don't have what we desire, and greed is the untamed eagerness to get what we desire, in abundance. Both of them easily lead to disaster as well as misfortune – even when we succeed to fulfill them. Especially when we fulfill them.

Turning discontent into its opposite is likely to involve actions that are harmful to others, and therefore at length to ourselves. But mainly, once we are filled with discontent, what could possibly cure it? It's most likely to linger on, whatever benefits we manage to gain. That beast, when awakened, is very difficult to put to sleep again.

To satisfy greed is a major feat that takes more than just one lifetime. Greed has no upper limit. When we are victims of it, the more we get the more we want. It's like a demon. Once it has appeared, there is no way of getting rid of it. Every offering to greed just makes it grow stronger. There is no fortune in the world large enough to bribe it off. So, even if the greedy one amasses a fortune, it will lead to nothing but misfortune.

Lao Tzu ends the chapter with a statement that we recognize: enough is enough is enough. You have to know what you really need, and decide that any more is unimportant, insignificant in spite of its splendor.

The Greek myth about King Midas says the same. His foremost wish was granted, when everything he touched turned into gold. Soon he discovered that this was true for food and drink as well. What is valuable is also very costly.

47

Without stepping out the door,
You can know the world.
Without looking through the window,
You can see Heaven's Way.
The longer you travel, the less you know.

Therefore:
The sage knows without traveling,
Perceives without looking,
Completes without acting.

Understanding without Exploring

Immanuel Kant, who lived in the 18th century, was one of the foremost of Western philosophers. He was born in the town Königsberg, and stayed there all his life. He had profound thoughts on god, life, peace, and just about everything else. As his philosophy got known around the world, everyone was amazed that so much could come out of a man who never in his life traveled more than ten miles from his home town.

Lao Tzu would have applauded his lifestyle. There is no need to explore every little corner of the world in order to understand how it works. There is not even a need to glare at it much. Its essence is obvious to anyone who is open to it.

You have it in yourself, too, so why go any further?

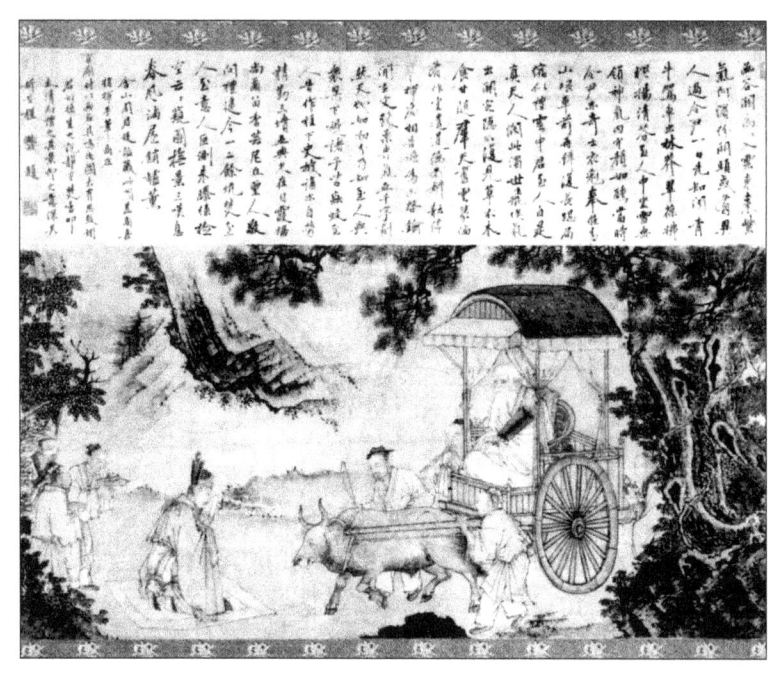

Lao Tzu meets the border guard Yin Hsi, who later convinces him to write the Tao Te Ching before leaving China.

Those who insist on searching it elsewhere are most likely to get lost.

We live in an era where science progresses by experimenting on things around us, as if our own beings and our own minds had nothing to do with it. But what is our world, without our presence in it? What does it look like through other eyes than ours?

Truly, whatever we discover about the universe and its mechanisms, it's still bound by how we experience it. Without our experience, we would not even be aware of the world around us.

In the time of Lao Tzu, and many centuries on, man was not removed from the world as if he were a mere observer of it. That makes sense. We are part of it, even when we observe it. So, our observations and conclusions depend on what we are, what we can see, and what we want everything to be. Science is completely objective only where its findings are of no importance to us.

So, Lao Tzu joins with Immanuel Kant, exploring the world through his mind and admitting it. Therefore, extensive travel is uncalled for. Wherever you travel, your mind follows. Actually, it's doing the traveling, so it leads. If you forget that, you flee from it. Then, what can you ever hope to understand?

This exploration, taking place inside instead of outside of us, is indeed another way of completing without acting. We find the truth by contemplation, not by chasing it with our instruments. Our present science will reach a point when this is again realized to be necessary.

Some scientific paradoxes, like those in Einstein's relativity and quantum physics, suggest that we have already gotten there.

As for Lao Tzu's use of the expression Heaven's Way instead of just the Way, see my comments on chapter 73.

48

Those who seek knowledge,
Collect something every day.
Those who seek the Way,
Let go of something every day.

They let go and let go,
Until reaching no action.
When nothing is done,
Nothing is left undone.

Never take over the world to tamper with it.
Those who want to tamper with it
Are not fit to take over the world.

Let Go

Letting go is a recurring theme in the *Tao Te Ching*. It's brought up in several chapters, for example the 19th, where I mention the similarity to Zen in this respect. In Zen, you let go to reach empty mind, a mental state of clarity, where nothing disturbs you or pulls you way from the soundness of the simple thought. There are many similarities between Zen and what Lao Tzu argues for.

Knowledge is a risky thing. It clogs the mind and makes it prejudiced. Those who seek it carry a load that gets heavier every day, and the chance of processing it to come to any conclusions diminishes. It's hard to be wise when you have too much to think about.

Following Tao, the Way, you learn to trust that it will

reveal the true workings of the world and everything in it. By leaning back and opening yourself to it, you watch Tao unfold in front of you, revealing itself from behind everything that happens. The chains of events have patterns, and these patterns show the fabric of Tao.

Letting go is also to become detached. It's not the same as indifference. You care and you have wishes, but you don't hurry to act before you are certain about the consequences of your actions. Otherwise you are very likely to do more harm than good.

Only do something when you really have to, and then only do that something. It will suffice.

Lao Tzu has so much fate in the perfection of Tao that he expects the occasions to be few, when action is needed. Mostly, things correct themselves, because they are governed by Tao. In Lao Tzu's mind, only people can at all deviate from the Way. Neither plants nor animals or any other things in our universe can.

Our Odd Nature

Actually, that's pretty much how modern science sees it, too. Dead things behave according to the laws of physics, plants and animals according to biology. They follow their nature. Only mankind has the nature that makes it possible for us to deviate from it. We shouldn't.

We are odd creatures, indeed. Not only can we deviate from nature, but we have a tendency to believe that we can improve it. That's absurd, especially since we are far from understanding it completely. Still, we want to take over the whole world and change it to our liking.

It's not only an ambition among the self-appointed dictators of which we've had far too many. It's almost a reflex of ours, existing in all of us. It starts as soon as we settle somewhere. In our children, it starts as soon as they can move their arms and hands at will. We want to make our marks, and we want to control the world down to every little detail.

That's exactly why we are not fit to rule the world, but that's also why we keep trying.

Even when we set out to correct our own mistakes and the misfortunes they created, we start again by seizing control of our surroundings and forcing changes on them. If we have damaged the world when taking power over it, we should not try to fix it with that same power, but lean back and let the world repair itself.

It will if we let it. Tao is the Way by which that comes about.

49

The sage has no concern for himself,
But makes the concerns of others his own.

He is good to those who are good.
He is also good to those who are not good.
That is the virtue of good.
He is faithful to people who are faithful.
He is also faithful to people who are not faithful.
That is the virtue of faithfulness.

The sage is one with the world,
And lives in harmony with it.
People turn their eyes and ears to him,
And the sage cares for them like his own children.

The Concern of the Sage

Tao Te Ching has great similarities with at least two other ideals – that of Zen and that of Christianity as expressed by Jesus in the Gospels. This chapter is a clear example of the latter.

There is reason for caution when finding similarities with what is part of one's own culture and tradition. We in the Western world have a tendency to compare everything we meet, no matter how exotic, with the concepts familiar to our own culture.

This is particularly true when we examine other religions and their gods. Actually, some of these traditions can only be called religions with quite a stretch of the imagination as well as the definition. The same is true for what we call gods.

But the similarities between the words of Jesus and those of Lao Tzu are so evident that I dare to point them out.

In this chapter, when Lao Tzu says that we should be good even to those who aren't, and that the sage cares for other people as if they were his own children, then it's almost as if he spoke the words of Jesus. Well, considering his seniority in time, it would be more correct to say that Jesus spoke as if quoting Lao Tzu. There are several chapters of the *Tao Te Ching* giving the same impression.

The self-sacrificing attitude Lao Tzu demonstrates in this chapter, is so familiar to our Christian tradition that there is no need for me to expand on it. We should set our own needs aside for the benefit of our fellow men. It's easier said than done. But if we all do it, Paradise on Earth is around the corner.

We should volunteer to show goodness and faith, without demanding the same in return. If such qualities are not unconditional, we remain in the paranoid world of everyone waiting for everyone else to lay down arms before we do so ourselves.

Lao Tzu describes this unselfishness as virtue, *te*, the second word in the title of his book. Virtue is the course of action, or non-action, necessary to live in accordance with the Way. It's not a method to reach success or praise, but it will lead to those things as well. Primarily, though, it's what should be done in order to accept what is natural.

It's what we do when we don't struggle to counter the natural course of things. That's why we mostly need to refrain from action, and accept what occurs.

50

We go from birth to death.
Three out of ten follow life.
Three out of ten follow death.
People who rush from birth to death
Are also three out of ten.
Why is that so?
Because they want to make too much of life.

I have heard that the one who knows how to live
Can wander through the land
Without encountering the rhinoceros or the tiger.
He passes the battlefield
Without being struck by weapons.
In him, the rhinoceros finds no opening for its horn.
The tiger finds no opening for its claws.
The soldiers find no opening for their blades.

Why is that so?
Death has no place in him.

How to Survive

How to live one's life is a complicated matter, occupying most of the *Tao Te Ching*. But also, merely to stay alive is difficult, and was even more so in the time of Lao Tzu. This chapter talks about how to survive at all.

Three out of ten follow life, which means that they reach old age. Three out of ten head for death. Lao Tzu probably refers to the tragedy of so many children not even reaching adulthood. Infant mortality was very high, actually all the way to the last couple of centuries, in China as well as in the Western world. The 30% should not be taken literally, but the figure was probably not that far from the truth.

Another three out of ten hurry from birth to death, in their desperation to make the most of it. Whether they actually die young because of it is not as significant as their incapacity to enjoy their lifespan. Whenever their death arrives, they will feel that life passed too quickly. That's the strange paradox of trying too hard to find the most time. It will slip away.

That makes nine out of ten. The tenth is the one who really knows how to relate to life, without desperation. What you cherish, but don't struggle too hard to keep, will not escape you. Life is like a cat. It enjoys your company if you don't try to enslave it and don't get too attached to it.

People who have this relaxed relation to life don't provoke death. Nor do they seek it. They walk through life with the spirit of a visitor, who enjoys the experience but doesn't for a moment expect it to last forever. They just live, as long as that is the case, and then they die when the time has come. They appreciate the former and accept the latter.

Without accepting death, they couldn't appreciate life. Without appreciating life, they could not accept death.

The killers of the world, whether they are animals, soldiers, or other threats, are not able to take aim at somebody who is indifferent. Such a person will not be made a target. To attack something, it has to have a defense. If not, then what to attack?

Those who know how to live don't display the intention of defending their lives by taking the lives of others, so they are no threats. Since they are unwilling to defend their lives, those lives seem to be of no value to others. Therefore others are not eager to take them.

Those who never consider taking the lives of others are no threats. So, there's no reason to attack them as some kind of preventive defense. Actually, only those who worry about death venture to impose it on others. And they are particularly anxious to do it on those who also fear death. Killing is mostly done for fear of death.

The ones who know how to live have no imminent fear of death. It's not something that governs their attitude or actions. Therefore it has no place in them. They just live when they live, and die when they die – like the rest of us, but without worrying so much about it.

51

The Way gives birth to them.
Virtue gives them nourishment.
Matter gives them shape.
Conditions make them whole.

Therefore:
Of all things,
None does not revere the Way and honor virtue.
Reverence of the Way and honoring virtue
Were not demanded of them,
But it is in their nature.

So, the Way gives birth to them,
Nourishes them,
Raises them,
Nurtures them,
Protects them,
Matures them,
Takes care of them.
It gives birth without seizing,
Helps without claim,
Fosters without ruling.
This is called the profound virtue.

All Things Are Nurtured

Tao as a source, out of which all things have come into existence, is mentioned several times in the *Tao Te Ching*. But virtue, *te*, giving them nourishment, is a somewhat confusing perspective. Human beings need virtue as nourishment for their character and perspectives on life. Perhaps the same thing can be said for the animals – but how can it be expected of plants and dead things?

What is hinted with the statement is either virtue as a kind of principle for the growth and development of all things, or some animistic standpoint, where everything in the world is connected and in some sense alive. Probably, it's a combination of both.

To Lao Tzu and his contemporaries, life was something other than it is to us. All of nature, with its movements, changes, and dynamics, could be seen as being alive. Movement is everywhere, so is growth and decay. Therefore, in many cultures it has been taken for granted that all things possess some kind of life. Otherwise, how could they change, and how could they be active, important parts of the human conditions?

We are enclosed in the world and we relate to it in countless ways, so it's definitely part of our lives. At least in that sense, the world is alive and bound to the same conditions as we are. The world is alive because it matters to our lives.

Also, since Lao Tzu sees Tao as something encompassing all, behind all, he gives equal omnipresence to virtue, the worldly manifestation of Tao. This relation between Tao and virtue is expressed by the last line of this chapter. How Tao behaves is called the profound virtue. So, Tao can be said to have virtue, therefore virtue must be present in everything born out of Tao.

Since Tao is the way things are and ought to be, it can be called virtuous. Tao is the original state of *Te*, virtue. The nature of Tao is virtuous, but not because it's bound by virtue. That would make it second. It's virtuous of itself, whereas the world coming out of it has virtue because of its origin, like genes transporting heredity from parents to children. The whole world and all things in it carry the virtue of Tao with them.

So, there is just one form of virtue, which is from Tao, and its essence is nothing but being in accordance with Tao. We are virtuous when we follow the Way.

52

The world's beginning is its mother.
To have found the mother
Is also to know the children.
Although you know the children,
Cling to the mother.
Until your last day you will not be harmed.

Seal the openings, shut the doors,
And until your last day you will not be exhausted.
Widen the openings, interfere,
And until your last day you will not be safe.

Seeing the small is called clarity.
Holding on to the weak is called strength.
Use the light to return to clarity.
Then you will not cause yourself misery.
This is called following the eternal.

Return to Clarity

The small and the seemingly weak are what truly rule the universe. This we know quite well from modern science. The characteristics and behavior of matter is decided by its smallest components, found in quantum physics.

The weakest of the basic forces is gravity, but in the large scale of the universe its power is vast enough to subdue anything. The small is the core, and the weak is what endures.

When Lao Tzu states that the light is the key to clarity,

we would like to think that he unknowingly refers to the importance of light and its speed in the theories of Einstein. That's hardly the case, although light has lately received significance beyond its symbolical use in ancient thought.

Light and Clarity

Light, *kuang*, may in Lao Tzu's use of it refer to Tao, the Way and the mother. Either it's the light in itself, or its patterns that can be found and examined in the light – when obstructions are removed and we are able to perceive the small. We need light to reach clarity.

Actually, the word used for clarity, *ming*, can also mean light, as well as brightness, brilliance, and understanding. We might use the word insight. Its pictogram is a combination of the sign for the sun and that of the moon. That's just about all the significant light found in the world, at the days of Lao Tzu.

Kuang means light, ray, brightness, brilliance, and shine. Originally, its pictogram showed a man carrying fire, in the form of a torch or something similar. This image suggests the idea that light should be brought and used in order to bring clarity to what we examine. By bringing light we see the things as they are, and thereby we reach clarity.

Safe, Not Saved

Another part of this chapter is also complicated to interpret: "until your last days you will not be safe." Traditionally, the last word has been understood and translated as "saved." This is an idea that seems far more Christian than Taoist.

In the 1990's, the oldest *Tao Te Ching* manuscript we have was found in Guodian. It dates back to around 300 BC. There, this sentence instead reads approximately: "you will

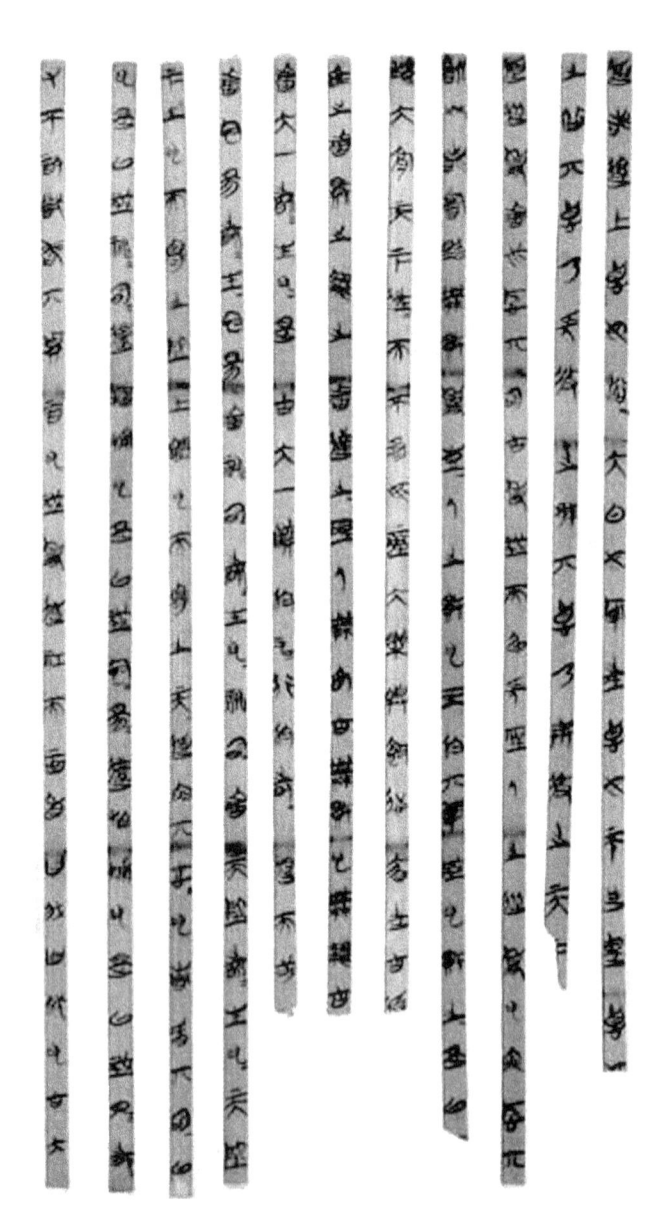

Tao Te Ching bamboo slips, found in Guodian. They are probably written around the year 300 BC, no later than 278 BC. The Guodian manuscript is the oldest one of Tao Te Ching found, so far.

not reach your last days," meaning that you will die before old age.

I settled for a compromise between the two, with the word "safe" instead of "saved." The meaning in the Guodian version and that of later versions meet somewhere there. If you open wide and meddle with your surroundings, you are at risk. That's true in many ways.

Sealing the openings and closing the doors can also be interpreted in several ways. Some claim that it points to the human senses, but Lao Tzu had enough humor also to imply the bodily cavities. Just like the soldier needs armor, every human being needs to take care and hold back, when appropriate. Also in our homes, there are many moments when we do best to keep our doors shut.

We should be careful with what we invite, and for what we open.

53

If I have just an ounce of sense,
I follow the great Way,
And fear only to stray from it.
The great Way is very straight,
But people prefer to deviate.

When the palace is magnificent,
The fields are filled with weeds,
And the granaries are empty.
Some have lavish garments,
Carry sharp swords,
And feast on food and drink.
They possess more than they can spend.
This is called the vanity of robbers.

It is certainly not the Way.

Robbery

Lao Tzu ends this chapter with what is also a joke. Robber, *tao*, is pronounced the same as Tao, the Way. But indeed, they are not the same. Lao Tzu deplores those who keep to themselves much more than they could ever consume. To him, that's robbery. Sadly, such robbers take pride in their gluttony.

In this respect, nothing has changed since the days of Lao Tzu. There are still those who have much more than they can spend, although they try hard with meaningless luxury, while there are many others who don't have even nearly enough. Those who follow the Way weep over this.

It must have been a daring statement by a man living in ancient China, where those who were rich had all the sharp swords at their command, and didn't hesitate to use them.

According to the legend, Lao Tzu wrote his book upon leaving the country for good. That may have given him the courage to be this outspoken. It's still impressive that such hard words about the ruling classes were passed on through the centuries.

Again, he speaks with a voice near that of Jesus, who said that it's more difficult for the rich to enter the kingdom of God than it is for a camel to pass through the eye of a needle. Their sense of humor in dealing with the subject is also related. But Jesus was not subsequently leaving the country, so his fate was a different one.

Those in power are quite touchy when their wealth and privileges are questioned.

54

What is well planted will not be uprooted.
What is well held will not escape.
Children and grandchildren will not cease to praise it.

Cultivate virtue in yourself,
And it will be true.
Cultivate virtue in the family,
And it will be overflowing.
Cultivate virtue in the town,
And it will be lasting.
Cultivate virtue in the country,
And it will be abundant.
Cultivate virtue in the world,
And it will be universal.

Therefore:
See others as yourself.
See families as your family.
See towns as your town.
See countries as your country.
See worlds as your world.

How do I know that the world is such?
By this.

Cultivate Virtue

The last line of this chapter is almost a riddle: "By this." The two words are not very explanatory. By what? The scholars have different ideas about it. The most likely answer is that Lao Tzu simply refers to what he has stated in the preceding lines of the chapter.

Chapter 21 ends with the same words.

Confucian Obligations

The world is like this, because the virtue of it connects all parts of it in the manner described. The chain from the individual through family, town, country, to the whole world, is quite Confucian.

Kung Tzu, Confucius, was according to legend contemporary with Lao Tzu, even slightly his junior. But it's at least as likely that it was the other way around. Taoism can be seen as a reaction to Confucianism. Whatever the case, there are some similarities among the many contradictions.

Confucianism stresses heavily the links of obligations one has towards family members and country.

But Lao Tzu is no friend of obligations. He prefers such bonds to be voluntary. They should be consequences of one's virtue, and one's sense of what's natural, and not some laws to which we are forced to surrender.

Virtue should be cultivated, and not preached. One needs to find it within oneself, in one's search for the Way. Otherwise, the virtue is ill planted and ill held, so it will be uprooted and escape.

Virtue only remains if it's reached by personal conviction. If it's demanded of us, we have no way of knowing if it's true, and then surely it will not be lasting.

Others as Yourself

When Lao Tzu says that you should see others as yourself, other families as your own, and so on, he doesn't necessarily mean that you must treat strangers with the same care you show the near and dear ones. It's possible that he says so, but it can also be a way of saying that other people, their needs and actions, can be understood by comparing to oneself.

If you want to understand others, you must start by understanding yourself. If you want to understand other countries, start by examining your own country.

It works the opposite way as well. If you want to understand yourself, compare with what you learn from watching others. It leads to the conclusion that you should treat others like you need to be treated. Again something that Jesus would agree with.

Lao Tzu might be slightly different from Jesus in how he motivates the principle. Although he wants us to be good, that's not the foremost issue in this chapter. Instead, he focuses on understanding the people involved and what virtue would apply.

It's a process of learning, more than one of compassion. It will lead to compassion, but without reaching it by learning, our compassion will be superfluous and misguided, just like our virtue will be if not firmly established according to Tao.

It's all a matter of cultivation. Virtue is no simple rule to memorize, but an endeavor of growing insight. It's a time consuming quest.

55

The one who is filled by virtue is like a newborn baby.
Wasps, scorpions, and serpents will not sting him.
Birds of prey and wild beasts will not strike him.
His bones are soft, his muscles weak,
But his grasp is firm.
He has not experienced the union of man and woman,
Still his penis rises.
His manhood is at its very height.
He can shout all day without getting hoarse.
His harmony is at its very height.

Harmony is called the eternal.
Knowing the eternal is called clarity.
Filling life exceedingly is called ominous.
Letting the mind control the vital breath is called force.

Things exalted then decay.
This is going against the Way.
What goes against the Way meets an early end.

The Virtue of the Infant

The first part of this chapter compares the sage to a newborn baby. Infants are soft and weak, yet their tiny hands grab with surprising firmness. Although they are many years away from puberty and sexual encounters, they get erections. They can scream forever, without getting hoarse, and with a shocking loudness at that.

　　Lao Tzu is obviously himself amused by the comparison, and by the paradoxes evident in babies. Indeed, they are inspirations to the sage.

It's not so that the virtuous should regress to the stage of the newborn. For example, there is no need to stay away from sexual experience. The infant erections are signs of manhood being present from the beginning, which is to say that a human being carries all of his or her potential already from the moment of birth.

Lao Tzu might also imply that the virtue of the innocent promotes potency. At least, most of us would agree that the sexual experience is enhanced if partaken in joyful and equal consent. That's the virtue of it.

The firm grasp of the virtuous is not to grab things for oneself, but for holding on to Tao and the noble principles by which it governs. Nor is the sage supposed to be shouting all day. Quite the contrary. But his voice of reason should not be easily silenced and good words should not escape him when called for.

As for the baby being invulnerable to vicious animals, it's possible that Lao Tzu is doing some wishful thinking. Actually, predators seem to prefer going after infants, since they are the easiest to catch and make the least resistance. Here, he might refer to the adult with a childishly pure mind, as mentioned in chapter 50. Those who know how to live, escape violent death because death has no place in them.

This can be said about newborn babies as well. Freshly born, they are full of life, and death is farther away from them than it will ever be.

The clarity that Lao Tzu speaks of in this chapter is the realization that harmony is eternal, because it meets with no resistance.

和 *Ho, harmony.*

The safest way to last is not to provoke resistance, from oneself as well as from others. Inner harmony means living at peace with oneself. Those who do are spared of frustrations, dissatisfaction, and depression. By living in harmony with your surroundings you avoid conflict and animosity. That's how harmony persists longer than the opposite.

The Chinese word for harmony, *ho*, also means peace and to be united. It's written with the sign for a grain or sprout, and that for the mouth. That's indeed an image of things in a delightful setting. The food meets the mouth. The resource meets the need.

Pushing Things
Filling life exceedingly and allowing the mind to control the vital breath are two examples of one and the same mistake – that of pushing things in life. There's no gain in overdoing things. It only invites bitter failure.

The vital breath, *ch'i* (or *qi*), is also mentioned in chapters 10 and 42. I explain it in some detail in the former of those chapters. This life energy flows readily through us and everything around us. It's a very natural thing, so if the mind tries to control it, the flow is disturbed and the vital breath might cease to function properly.

That doesn't mean it should not be used. It is used, automatically, when we intend to do something, when we concentrate on something, and so on. Our bodies have access to it. When we act, it will be there according to our needs, if we just allow the natural process to have its course. But if our minds try to produce and control the vital breath, there is a risk that we block that flow.

It's also an indication that we might try to misuse it. When the vital breath is forced, it tends to be destructive and malign instead of healing.

Decay Follows

The last three lines of the chapter are exactly the same as in chapter 30, where they don't fit as well. Maybe some copyist along the way accidentally doubled it. In the oldest existing *Tao Te Ching* manuscript, found in Guodian, the lines are missing in chapter 30.

In this chapter, the three lines fit very well. They come right after Lao Tzu warns against filling life exceedingly and forcing the vital breath. Those are two examples of exalting things by overdoing them. Decay must follow.

What has reached its highest point must then descend. That's as true in life as it is in drama and the movies. If we hurry to that moment, we only manage to shorten our lives.

Still, every one of us would like to have life reach a wondrous height before we leave it. No one would be pleased by having that peak experience early and then spend the rest of a long life reminiscing, nor would we be comfortable to take our last breath without ever having reached it.

Ideal life is similar to drama in so many ways. So, we need to have the climax very near the end. Otherwise, what is there to long for in the inevitable future?

56

Those who know it do not speak about it.
Those who speak about it do not know it.

Seal the openings.
Shut the doors.
Dull the sharpness.
Untie the knots.
Dim the light.
Become one with the dust.
This is called the profound union.

Those who obtain it
Can neither be seduced nor abandoned.
Those who obtain it
Can neither be favored nor neglected.
Those who obtain it
Can neither be honored nor humiliated.
Therefore, they are the most esteemed in the world.

Integrity

This chapter connects to two others. Sealing the openings and shutting the doors is also mentioned in chapter 52, as how to avoid exhausting yourself in life.

Dulled sharpness, untied knots, dimmed light, and becoming one with the dust, are stated in chapter 4 as qualities of Tao, the Way. Since it's the manner of Tao, we should try to obtain it.

The profound union is that with Tao and the world of its

道德經

design. Thereby one becomes united with nature and the natural Way of things.

Those who obtain this union can't be seduced, since nothing that they should avoid would tempt them. Nor are they abandoned, since they are not dependent on anyone or anything out of their own reach. This independence makes them indifferent to favors and unafraid of neglect. They seek no honor and wave it off if it's still bestowed on them. That makes them impossible to humiliate as well.

Ambition is the will for more than what is at one's immediate grasp. Without ambition there is little that one might find missing, and disappointment is unlikely. Few privileges would overtrump that. The most esteemed persons are those that didn't seek esteem.

Those qualities can be summarized into one: integrity. By sealing the openings and shutting the doors, integrity is reached. The humble course follows naturally. You feel no need to make noise and receive recognition, no need for sharpness or shine. You are pleased with what you are and what you have, because you are sure to be it and have it.

Integrity makes you immune to seduction as well as abandonment. You need no favors and are not upset by neglect. Being honored by others doesn't flatter you and you're not embarrassed by efforts to humiliate you. You may be worthy of the most esteem in the world, but you don't care.

Integrity begins by recognizing one's own identity, and remains by not wishing to change it.

The first two lines are also signs of integrity. What you really know, you don't need to brag about, so you make no speeches. Those who do, need to pretend to know what they are unsure about. They never stop talking.

In several versions of the *Tao Te Ching*, the first two lines lack the indication of a certain subject, so they read: "Those who know don't speak, those who speak don't know." But the oldest manuscripts found, the one from Guodian and the two from Mawangdui, include an "it" that is most certainly Tao, the Way.

That's the fundamental knowledge, which can only be obtained by someone who thereby is not eager to proclaim it. Also, since it's so fundamental, others can't refrain from claiming to know, with so many words, although they are far from certain.

57

Use justice to rule a country.
Use surprise to wage war.
Use non-action to govern the world.

How do I know it is so?
As for the world,
The more restrictions and prohibitions there are,
The poorer the people will be.
The more sharp weapons people have in a country,
The bigger the disorder will be.
The more clever and cunning people are,
The stranger the events will be.
The more laws and commands there are,
The more thieves and robbers there will be.

Therefore the sage says:
I do not act,
And people become reformed by themselves.
I am at peace,
And people become fair by themselves.
I do not interfere,
And people become rich by themselves.
I have no desire to desire,
And people become like the uncarved wood by themselves.

People Can Govern Themselves

Some translators of the *Tao Te Ching* presume that the first three lines of this chapter say what not to do and what to do. Justice and surprise are inferior, and only non-action, *wu-wei*, is in accordance with Tao. I think that's too harsh a judgment.

Lao Tzu is not unrealistic, nor is he impractical. For ruling the country, justice is a reasonable ideal. For winning wars, surprise is a commendable strategy. That's all fine, considering the limited perspectives involved. But for governing the world, only non-action will do.

He is not dismissing the two former methods, since they are relevant in connection to their objects. He just reminds us that on a larger scale, and for truly lasting purposes, we need to return to Tao and its principles.

In the following, he specifies what terms apply to the grand perspective. In the world as a whole, and in a government that wishes to last, restrictions and prohibitions just lead to poverty. That will have its recoils. That's where justice fails. An armed population and preparations for war will cause calamity. Weapons have that consequence. So much for military strategy.

Furthermore, when people are clever and scheming, there's no way of telling what will happen. The surprises will be far greater than any warlord might come up with. And for each new law there will be many more people committing crimes, both such that had not been illegal beforehand and such that always were. The smaller the pasture, the more of the livestock will jump the fence.

道德經

So, the sage leans back and avoids doing the least bit more than what is absolutely called for. That's much less than most leaders ever imagine. People search for norms and make their own decent rules, when not cornered by laws. A multitude of laws mostly triggers disobedience and the search for loopholes.

The uncarved wood is a frequently used metaphor for a pure and simple mind. For people to conform to it, their leaders have to do the same. It starts by the leaders admitting that they are not different from the ones to be led.

Lao Tzu also points out, playing with words as is his habit, that a leader must be free of desire. He stresses it by doubling it. Desire, if just restrained, is still desire. One must be free of the desire to desire.

Many versions of the *Tao Te Ching* only have one occurrence of the word in the last sentence of this chapter, but the oldest manuscripts, that from Guodian and those from Mawangdui, use the double. The pun was probably present in the original version.

Truth also needs a laugh. Remember what Lao Tzu says in chapter 41. Without the laughter it would not be Tao.

58

When the government is quite unobtrusive,
People are indeed pure.
When the government is quite prying,
People are indeed conniving.

Misery is what happiness rests upon.
Happiness is what misery lurks beneath.
Who knows where it ends?
Is there nothing correct?
Correct becomes defect.
Good becomes ominous.
People's delusions have certainly lasted long.

Therefore the sage is sharp but does not cut,
Pointed but does not pierce,
Forthright but does not offend,
Bright but does not dazzle.

What to Trust?

We are never closer to misery than when we are happy. The one so easily turns into the other. They are strongly linked, and mutually dependent. Were it not for happiness, misery would not exist, and the other way around. So, it's not always evident which is which.

What was correct can suddenly prove to be completely wrong. It happens all the time in science. It's not rare in politics and philosophy either. The same uncertainty can be found in ethics. What's right today may be dead wrong to-

The Te sign in three old versions (oracle, bronze, and seal), and in its present form.

morrow. What seems to be good can threaten to do a lot of harm.

The future is as vague as the true state of the present. We don't know where we are going, because we don't really know where we are.

Since mankind stands on such shaky ground, it would be rude and obtrusive of the sage to shout commands, declare conclusions, and point in an exact direction. People don't follow willingly when they feel forced, and they can't understand what they are not allowed to examine by themselves.

The sage can gently give clues and appropriate suggestions, without demanding compliance. No more.

Governments should do the same. Even if they are certain of knowing what's best for everybody, it will not be accomplished if done by force. People will react and resist.

That might seem almost self-destructive, but the damage would be more severe and profound if people allowed themselves to be led on the Way, as if they were sheep. They are not, so they need to find their own way, even if that should lead them away from Tao. Otherwise they can never know when they happen to step on the right track.

We don't walk on the Way with our feet only. We must be there with our whole beings, including our minds and hearts. So, it has to be voluntary, and the progress must be felt inside, instead of just proclaimed from above. We simply have to do it ourselves, each and every one of us.

This is explained in chapters 18 and 38. Force is the worst, then rituals, then righteousness, then benevolence, then virtue, and above them all is Tao. It's impossible to lead people to Tao by force, almost as impossible to do it with rituals, and just slightly more possible with righteousness.

Benevolence could almost do the trick, but not if it's turned into one of the others. It usually is. Benevolence is often used as an excuse for force, although force can never be benevolent.

59

When leading people and serving Heaven,
Nothing exceeds moderation.
Truly, moderation means prevention.
Prevention means achieving much virtue.

When much virtue is achieved,
Nothing is not overcome.
Nothing not overcome means
Nobody knows the limits.
When nobody knows the limits,
One can rule the country.

The one who rules like the mother lasts long.
This is called deep roots and a solid base,
the Way to long life and clarity.

Rule with Moderation

A leader serving Heaven tries to rule in accordance with nature, following Tao, the Way. Moderation is the key. One should not interfere more than necessary, not act if not sure of how, and not overdo things. There is no feat so great that its good exceeds the benefit of reluctance to perform great feats.

When moderation is used, there is sensitivity to actual needs and there are remaining resources to deal with them, should they appear. Also, with a moderate perspective, one becomes aware of problems while they are still small. If you want to act as little as possible, you see the small things that need to be considered and dealt with. A wise leader has no longing to cause revolutions, but pays attention to detail.

The preventive perspective is indeed in accordance with Tao, and therefore it constantly increases virtue. The leader becomes nobler, and so does the people. Sensible leadership promotes sensibility.

Wherever there are leaders – in the family, in the workplace, in the community, or in the whole country – everybody matures from the leader's example and becomes wiser by following the leader's directions. So, when the leadership is done with ease, it will all the time get easier.

Since virtue is in accordance with Tao, everything gets easier along the Way, and there is no limit as to what can be solved or accomplished.

If the leader knows how to act and when not to act, there is nothing that cannot be overcome. Even if people are not aware of why this is so, they will feel it, take comfort in it, and respect the leadership. They will voluntarily submit to it and support it. Then it's possible to rule the whole country.

Even the mightiest ruler needs the approval of the people, at the very least its acceptance. No quantity of weaponry and soldiers will do as a substitute. People are sure to approve of a leader who seems to have limitless ability. With such a leader they feel safe.

Sadly, this might be the case even if the leader is heading towards disaster.

No matter how powerful and massively supported, the worthy leader must rule like a mother. Lao Tzu surely refers to the mother of all, which is Tao, but also to the motherly fashion of leadership. It's based on care and yielding, on acting with caution and consideration.

The mother works for her children, and not for her own benefit. It may not be true for every mother who ever lived, but it's certainly the principle of Tao, the mother of all. Therefore, anyone being motherly in that fashion will be saluted, supported, and successful.

That's the Way by which to last for long and find clarity.

60

Ruling a great country is like cooking a small fish.

When the world is ruled according to the Way,
The ghosts lose their power.
The ghosts do not really lose their power,
But it is not used to harm people.

Not only will their power not harm people,
Nor will the sage harm people.
Since neither of them causes harm,
Unified virtue is restored.

The Ghosts Approve

The ghosts, *kuei*, were the restless spirits of deceased ancestors, according to beliefs at the time of Lao Tzu. That's quite the same as what we mean by ghosts. And just like this chapter says, we foster the idea that the ghosts are only harmful if they are displeased. If the country is ruled wisely, in accordance with the Way, the ghosts will not be upset.

Lao Tzu is probably not indicating that a country ruled according to Tao becomes invulnerable to the power of the ghosts, and they definitely don't lose it. They just cease to bring harm to people. If the country should go back to deviating from the Way, the ghosts will surely bring harm again.

The sage, too, will bring no harm to people if the country is ruled according to Tao. That seems self-evident. When the country is on the right path, there is no need for inter-

Kuei, ghost.

ference of any kind, whether it would be harmful or beneficial. The sage knows this well.

What Lao Tzu implies with these words is that the sage might very well bring harm to people, if the country is heading the wrong way. Even if the sage again were to do nothing, the situation would be harmful.

People suffer in a country with a bad ruler. They will suffer more, during the process of correcting things. Such suffering is unavoidable.

Sadly, it's also necessary. That's the harm the sage might bring: the need for costly reform and painful action, like the pruning of twigs and branches in order to keep a tree healthy.

This is avoided if the country is ruled wisely, in accordance with Tao. Then the ghosts will not be upset, so they will do no harm, and the sage doesn't need to promote dire measures. The virtue of the ghosts and that of the sage are united, working for a common good.

The idea of the ghosts being pleased or upset doesn't need to be taken literally, for us to find it relevant. We don't have to believe in ghosts. But just as we consider what future is in store for our children and theirs, we should contemplate what our ancestors expected from us, and what they would have thought about how we handle the greatest of gifts – the world they handed over to us.

61

A great country is like the lower outlet of a river.
It is the world's meeting ground, the world's female.

The female always surpasses the male with stillness.
In her stillness she is yielding.

Therefore:
If a great country yields to a small country,
It will conquer the small country.
If a small country yields to a great country,
It will be conquered by the great country.
So, some who yield become conquerors,
And some who yield get conquered.

A great country needs more people to serve it.
A small country needs more people to serve.
So, if both shall get what they need,
The great country ought to yield.

Conquer by Yielding

Water flows to the river's outlet, because it's low, because it's the point that yields the most. To Lao Tzu, yielding is foremost a female quality, alike the mother of all, which is Tao. What yields the most attracts the rest of the world.

Another symbol for it would be the sea or lake at which the river ends. The water that flowed so eagerly to get there is absorbed and becomes as still as that great body of water it joined.

So is a big country. It attracts and absorbs its surroundings, without being stirred by this. And so is the female quality, the mother, who in her yielding stillness overcomes the male nature. Movement is calmed by stillness, and force is useless against the yielding.

Now, a great country should not need aggression and force to conquer smaller countries. A yielding stillness is enough. Its size will make smaller countries succumb to it, like the river water flows into the sea. We have seen it a lot through history. Great kingdoms devour small ones, without even trying. They do it by their size alone, as if the force at work were gravity.

Even if a small country momentarily succeeds in conquering a great one, it can only lead to the latter taking over the former. If they are joined, no matter how, it cannot end any other way than with the small country becoming part of the great country.

So, there's never cause for the great country to do other than yield.

Small countries yielding, on the other hand, will quickly be overtaken by great ones. To withstand the natural pull and growth of the great country, they would need to resist actively and constantly. It's not easy, and it's not without dire costs. Of course, trying to conquer the great country by force is equally futile. The only thing a small country can do, when neighboring a great one, is to isolate itself, which also takes its toll.

We have seen it recently in our world, and see it still. Small countries bordering to great ones close those borders firmly, not to be overcome in one way or other. These borders are not only the walls built between the countries and guarded by soldiers. There are cultural borders as well, locking out all possible influence from the great country, also trade walls and diplomatic ones.

Such small countries become isolated islands where progress is halted, and people are stuck to life as it was in the past. It's doomed not to last, but if the leadership is fanatic about this isolation, reform will take time and the road to it will be painful.

What small countries really need, is to participate in both the flow towards the great country and the influence that comes the other way. A country that is lost by doing so, was not much of a country to begin with.

Participation leads to gain, for the small as well as the great country. Small countries will grow if they get more people to serve, whether that's inside our outside their borders. Great countries need lots of people to keep them running.

When people are allowed to comply, wherever they live, things solve themselves. Small countries prosper, because they get more tasks to perform. Great countries prosper, because they get more resources by which to prevail.

So, the only thing that benefits both countries is for the great one to do what is natural for it, which is to yield. If the great country refuses to yield, but conquers with force, it cannot keep at length what it seized. When yielding, the great country still conquers, but because this benefits also the conquered, a lasting harmony will ensue.

62

The Way is the source of all things,
Good people's treasure and bad people's refuge.

Fine words are traded.
Noble deeds gain respect.
But people who are not good,
Why abandon them?

So, when the emperor is crowned
Or the three dukes are appointed,
Rather than sending a gift of jade
Carried by four horses,
Remain still and offer the Way.

Why did the ancients praise the Way?
Did they not say it was because you find what you seek
And are saved from your wrongdoings?
That is why the world praises it.

The Greatest Gift

This chapter is partly rather confusing. The division of people into good and bad is not as convincingly Taoist as, say, comparing their distance to Tao, the Way. But they might refer to the same thing.

Lao Tzu is clear about those close to Tao being good, so maybe those far away from it can be called bad. Still, it would be more accurate to call them lost, like someone leaving the road and getting too deep into the forest.

There's also an interesting difference in what Tao is to the good and the bad: a treasure to the former and a refuge to the latter. It indicates that the good are able to use their understanding of Tao, whereas the others depend on it for their well-being. One is active, the other passive.

This is repeated later in the chapter, where it says that Tao saves you from wrongdoings.

It's a message of forgiveness. Tao is like a mother also to those who have turned away from it. None is abandoned. Those who speak fine words and do noble deeds get their rewards, so they should do fine. But it would be cruel to abandon those who are unable of the same, those who don't shine.

Caring For All

Therefore, the first thing that the emperor should receive when crowned is the understanding of Tao and the compassion it promotes.

So should the three dukes, *san-kung*. This important trio of ancient China consisted of the Grand Preceptor, the Grand Mentor, and the Grand Guardian. In later versions of the *Tao Te Ching* they were changed to the three ministers, *san-ch'ing*, those of education, war, and work, because they became more important in the government of China.

Rulers on all levels must understand that society can only improve if all its inhabitants are guided. If just the ones who already behave decently are cared for, the others will soon cause tremendous problems. When they are deserted and damned, the only thing remaining for them is to revolt.

Caring for the bad as well as the good is not only the compassionate thing to do. It's also the most practical.

63

Act without action.
Pursue without interfering.
Taste the tasteless.

Make the small big and the few many.
Return animosity with virtue.
Meet the difficult while it is easy.
Meet the big while it is small.

The most difficult in the world
Must be easy in its beginning.
The biggest in the world
Is small in its beginning.
So, the sage never strives for greatness,
And can therefore accomplish greatness.

Lightly given promises
Must meet with little trust.
Taking things lightly
Must lead to big difficulties.
So, the sage regards things as difficult,
And thereby avoids difficulty.

Big Is Small at First

We already know about non-action, *wu-wei*, and about the importance of avoiding to interfere, but what about tasting the tasteless?

Well, chapter 12 says that the five flavors dull the

mouth. Spicy food is tiresome at length. Fireworks in the mouth deafen the palate. Chapter 12 also warns against a multitude of colors and tones. Spectacles are fun at first, but at length they dull the senses.

Tasting the tasteless is to increase one's sensitivity by being restrictive with stimuli. Sensations wear down the senses. When you increase your sensitivity you learn to taste what seems tasteless. You perceive nuance and observe the small things.

With increased sensitivity the small things grow in your perception of them, and you discover their importance. This is another way of saying what was stated in chapter 59: moderation means prevention. When you see the glimpses and listen to whispers, you become aware of things at the moment of their appearance.

They may be small and seem completely insignificant. But if you contemplate their possible consequences at length, you may be able to avoid disaster.

That's meeting the big while it's still small. Anyone with huge responsibilities must learn it, or crisis after crisis will appear.

Big problems start as small problems. That's when to solve them. Big obstacles start as small obstacles. That's when to overcome them.

This is true for one's personal life, as well as for the family, the town, the country, and the whole world. Whatever great problem we live with, if we look back we discover that it could have been solved easily in the beginning. But at that time nobody cared.

We are often stuck in the misconception that the world is a static place, although we can see that everything in it moves and changes constantly. When problems appear, they are usually quite small and nonthreatening. So we ignore them, thinking that they will stay that size forever. They don't.

Any problem not dealt with will grow. That's the way it is. We need to learn to deal with problems immediately. Then we will find that we need to do almost nothing.

Actually, many problems are initially so small that they are solved just by recognizing them. By discovering and exposing them, we make our world immune to their potential harm.

In the middle of his reasoning about big and small, Lao Tzu states that we should return animosity with virtue. That attitude alone would solve just about any major crisis in society, if it had been applied early on. Animosity feasts on being met by animosity. If not, it will wither.

So, to create a peaceful world we must learn not to respond to aggression with the same, but treat it in a noble manner. That's great virtue, in the sense of being morally superior as well as being the most efficient countermeasure.

Treating small issues as if they were big, is learning to take things seriously. Not only should we seriously consider what we want to do before doing it, but also what seems so insignificant that we feel no urge at all to deal with it. The danger lies in ignorance and indifference – especially in the latter.

In society, few things are as damaging as indifference.

64

Stillness is easy to maintain.
What has not yet emerged is easy to prevent.
The brittle is easy to shatter.
The small is easy to scatter.
Solve it before it happens.
Order it before chaos emerges.

A tree as wide as a man's embrace
Grows from a tiny shoot.
A tower of nine stories
Starts with a pile of dirt.
A climb of eight hundred feet
Starts where the foot stands.

Those who act will fail.
Those who seize will lose.
So, the sage does not act and therefore does not fail,
Does not seize and therefore does not lose.
People fail at the threshold of success.
Be as cautious at the end as at the beginning.
Then there will be no failure.

Therefore the sage desires no desire,
Does not value rare treasures,
Learns without learning,
Recovers what people have left behind.
He wants all things to follow their own nature,
But dares not act.

The Sage Dares Not Act

The first half of this chapter adds arguments to what was explained in the previous one: the importance of solving problems before they grow big.

The connection to chapter 63 is so obvious that one must wonder why they are divided. The reason might be one of length. Chapter 63 is long enough as it is, without the first half of this chapter. Together they would form a chapter longer by far than any other in the *Tao Te Ching*.

We are reminded of the fact that the division of the text into 81 chapters is a later revision. It was done several centuries after the book was written. The only division assumed to be original was that into two parts: chapters 1-37, called *Tao*, and 38-81, called *Te*.

The last line that deals with the theme of the previous chapter is the one about a climb of eight hundred feet. Most versions of it read differently: "A journey of a thousand *li* starts where you stand." But both the manuscripts found in Mawangdui, dating to around 200 BC, have lines similar to the one used here.

The manuscript from Guodian, a hundred years older, is inconclusive on this point, because of damages to it.

I can understand why the line was changed somewhere along the way. The line above it already introduces height, so length would make more sense to deal with next. Still, I have decided to go with what is so far established as the oldest version.

The two versions make no difference in meaning. Projects of whatever size are minute at the moment they begin.

Attention to the End

The second half of this chapter deals with the danger of action. What is done is hard to undo, so it has to be considered very seriously beforehand.

Lao Tzu actually claims that most actions fail, if not all of them. Only if there is just as much care about the end as the beginning, there is a chance of success. That really means the same care all through.

That might seem self-evident, but it's easily neglected. We tend to start our projects with resolute energy and complete attention, but soon our concentration wavers and our efforts decrease. It's as if we tire quickly. Or we might have the illusion that things we start reach their completion automatically, as if nothing can go wrong along the way. It may be a combination of both.

Our behavior is bound by patterns inside our minds. The habit we have of starting things and then just letting them go, stems from the patterns of how we think about the world.

It's the rhythm of existence: We give life to our children, take care of them while they need it to survive, and then let them go – beyond the future that we can ourselves expect to reach. Probably, we tend to see all our projects as children of ours, and therefore lack the urge to follow them through to the end. We might not even want them to ever end.

It's strange how human deeds are slowed down right before completion. The last steps of a long walk are not the quickest. At the end of a meal we chew less eagerly than when the plate was full. The end of a song is rarely as abrupt as its beginning. We hurry into things but hesitate when the end comes near.

In many cases there are obvious reasons for this. Still, it's a pattern we follow, even when there's no reason for it. We like beginnings but fear endings.

Surely, this has to do with the fact that we will all die, and we know it. A start is like birth, an end is like death. We cheer the former and dread the latter. Lao Tzu has told us that we should not hurry from the one to the other, and we rarely do – willingly. So, we have great trouble finishing things of any kind.

Because of our unwillingness to deal with endings, we are prone to fail with what we begin.

Shortcomings of the Sage

The sage has such respect for this shortcoming of ours, he refrains from action. He desires no desire, seeks no treasure, ignores knowledge, and settles for what others reject. He has no ambition. He dares not act, although he is wise enough to lead the world around him on its natural course.

He must suspect that he, too, has the shortcomings he finds in others, at least when it comes to action. So, in his wisdom he refrains from acting.

In many versions of the *Tao Te Ching*, the last lines of this chapter read: "He lets all things follow their own nature, and dares not act." This implies that the sage is afraid of disturbing the good order, and therefore refrains from action.

Again, the Mawangdui manuscripts present another reading: "He could help all things follow their own nature, but dares not act." It's supported by the Guodian manuscript. I have allowed myself a small compromise, with the word 'wants' instead of 'could help,' which is sort of halfway to 'lets.'

Still, the difference is considerable. It means that although the sage sees the need for improvement, he holds still. If interfered with, even an imperfect world risks getting worse. Also when things don't go the right way, there's an additional risk in trying to correct them.

Usually, our excuse for springing into action is that there's need for improvement. There certainly is, in many cases. Still, that's no guarantee we will not make things worse. The risk is actually increased. We easily find the right course of action in a well ordered world, but how to sort out a mess?

To find the right solution, we must know where it leads and how it will end. Our discomfort with endings makes us badly equipped for that.

65

In ancient times,
Those who followed the Way
Did not try to give people knowledge thereof,
But kept them ignorant.
People are difficult to rule
Because of their knowledge.

To rule by knowledge ravages the country.
To rule not by knowledge blesses the country.
To understand these two is to have precept.
To always have precept is called profound virtue.

Profound virtue is indeed deep and wide.
It leads all things back to the great order.

No Rule by Knowledge

In any Eastern culture, when ancient times are mentioned, it's always to point out what would be commendable and wise. The idea that past times were superior to the present is found just about everywhere, even in the Western world prior to the scientific revolution, a few hundred years ago.

Actually, it's only the last hundred years or so that we have changed significantly into regarding the past as dark and the present as bright. About the future, though, opinions are mixed.

Lao Tzu was definitely in support of praising his past as superior to his present. He makes it clear in several lines of the *Tao Te Ching*. In the distant past, people were nobler and wiser, following Tao, the Way, more closely. It made sense to him, since the ancestors lived nearer to the very emergence of the world through Tao. Not much had been corrupted, yet.

Also, there were several classics, *ching*, written by excellent minds, already at his time. He probably saw few contemporary books, except his own, which were possible to compare to the old ones. His conclusion could be none other than the deterioration of the human mind in general and human virtue in particular.

So, when he starts this chapter saying that the sages of ancient times didn't convey their knowledge of the Way to other people, he must mean that it was a wise choice of theirs. People were kept ignorant, so that they were easier to rule. Otherwise, the country's stability and order were at risk.

Why This Book?

It's strange, somewhat contradicting other messages of his book, that Lao Tzu praises hiding from people even the understanding of Tao. For one thing, why then would he write a book explaining it?

But knowledge of Tao is not necessarily understanding it or being able to follow it. Insufficient knowledge can even be an obstacle. People think they know, so they close their eyes and get no closer to Tao. They settle with having a name for it. This may be the kind of knowledge that Lao Tzu wants to keep away from people.

Actually, most knowledge is like that. Each phenomenon in nature is given a name, as is every plant and animal. That doesn't mean we understand them, nor does it mean that we are clear about their roles in the world.

Still, those who want to appear learned make sure to memorize a lot of such names, and thereby claim to have a perfect understanding of the things named. Already in the first chapter of the *Tao Te Ching* we are told that this is a mistake.

Tao is not just a road you walk, and its name doesn't reveal its essence.

Lao Tzu complains in chapter 32: "There are already many names. One must know when it's enough." He should have had a glimpse of our time. It would shock him. Today, we have so many more names on so many more things, but we still fail to understand how they are connected, and what ultimate law they obey.

We should halt the naming, and start our quest for the truth behind all things. That's what Lao Tzu talks about in his book. In the absence of the truth he prefers that people are ignorant, not caring for knowledge.

Democracy
But it's difficult to deny that Lao Tzu also genuinely doubts educating the masses. The more people know, the more they will interfere with government. Although Lao Tzu is compassionate about the well-being of the people, he knows nothing about democracy.

At the time he lived, there were experiments with it so far away from his abode that he had no way of hearing about it. Ancient Greece had no contact with China, where the democratic idea was unthinkable.

In a democracy, the people's knowledge is essential. Without it, there's just the pretense of democracy. People need to know as much as their elected leaders do, or they will be powerless against them.

On the other hand, in a kingdom or an empire like that of ancient China, people should be powerless, not to interfere with the ruler's plans. Then they should be kept ignorant. It's not the ideal state by far, but Lao Tzu and his contemporaries saw no alternative.

As for our time, being one where democracy is somewhat established and cultured, profound virtue should be explained to people, so that it encompasses all of them. That's how a democracy can be properly governed, since everybody has a role in it.

Today, Tao and its virtue need to be learned by all, or our society will surely fail. So, now Lao Tzu would probably agree that his book is called for.

66

The river and the sea can be kings of a hundred valleys,
Because they lie below them.
That is why they can be the kings of a hundred valleys.

Therefore:
If the sage wants to stand above people,
He must speak to them from below.
If he wants to lead people,
He must follow them from behind.

Therefore:
When the sage stands above people,
They are not oppressed.
When he leads people,
They are not obstructed.
The world will exalt him
And not grow tired of him.

Because he does not resist,
None in the world resists him.

Go Low to Stand High

When Lao Tzu says that there are things that can rule over valleys, it comes as a surprise. He frequently compares Tao to the valley, and who can rule Tao? But the rivers float downwards and the sea is lower than the land, so they behave like Tao in their yielding. By their humble yielding they can become rulers.

The sage knows very well to do the same. When he rises above people, he speaks to them as from below, like a servant and not a king. When leading them in a certain direction, he walks behind them, as if following their initiative.

The art of leadership is not to be obvious about it. People are happy to obey someone who makes his or her orders into questions, instead of exclamations.

It's not just an attitude, like acting on a stage. It needs to be accompanied by certain principles of leadership, striving not to increase people's burdens, but to diminish them.

Power includes the ability to treat others hurtfully and make decisions that oppose their interests. The good leader should struggle hard to avoid such actions. The welfare of the people should always be the leader's primary concern.

Following behind people, instead of being an obstruction in front of them, also means being sensitive to their needs. Merely hiding in the back of the line, right after pointing the way, is not enough.

The good leader should always be sensitive to where people really want to go, what directions they favor and which ones they want to avoid. That's following behind.

Always Several Options

It's still an active leadership. Most of all, the ruler gets to choose which one of several options will be pursued. There are always several options. When making the choice, the good leader considers people's welfare and the wishes they might have in their hearts. Other considerations are secondary.

The least important aspect is the leader's personal interest.

People resist a leader who resists or ignores their interests. A leader, who makes it clear that what benefits the people is what's first on the agenda, will not be opposed. How can you oppose someone who is devoted to work on what's best for you?

Such leaders are rare, so we would all make sure to obey and respect them.

67

The whole world says that my Way is great like nothing else.
It is great because it is like nothing else.
If it were like everything else,
It would long ago have become insignificant.

I have three treasures that I cherish.
The first is compassion.
The second is moderation.
The third is not claiming to be first in the world.

By compassion one can be brave.
By moderation one can be generous.
By not claiming to be first in the world one can rule.

But to be brave without compassion,
Generous without moderation,
And rule without refraining from being first in the world
Are certain deaths.

So, those who have compassion when they do battle
Will be victorious.
Those who likewise defend themselves
Will be safe.
Heaven will rescue and protect them with compassion.

Battle with Compassion

In the beginning of this chapter, Lao Tzu plays with the word *hsiao*, which means both 'like' and 'small.' The latter

I dared to translate as 'insignificant,' to clarify what kind of small Lao Tzu refers to here. The two words have different pictograms, but they are pronounced the same.

With his little joke, he implies that something bearing a likeness to other things has to be small. It certainly makes sense in relation to significance. What looks like a lot of other things loses its significance. But size is not affected in the same manner.

What is true regarding size, though, is that the smaller things are, the more difficult it is for our eyes to tell them apart. Who can separate one mosquito from another? Who even cares? Our eyes prefer to focus on big things, and we tend to regard them as important, judging just by their size.

The lines about size and significance are very likely to be a separate chapter in the eyes of the author. They have little to do with what follows, or for that matter how the previous chapter ends.

Vital Qualities

Next, Lao Tzu talks about the three qualities he regards as the most important: compassion, moderation, and reluctance to be first in the world. The last we can describe as modesty. Compassion leads to bravery, moderation to generosity, and modesty to the ability to rule. They contain the seeds to what are practically their opposites.

Of far greater importance is that these opposites are in dire need of the three qualities, or they lead to disaster.

Bravery without compassion is what can be seen in soldiers with no care for the lives they take, or self-appointed heroes who bully people around them for no other reason than that they can. Inconsiderate bravery is indeed disastrous, sooner or later also to the ones expressing it.

Generosity without moderation leads to meaningless waste. It's gluttony, and no fortune is so great that it will not be spent, eventually. It's also provocative. Even those who benefit from such generosity are offended by it. Whatever they get from it, they are at the same time reminded of their own lack of resources.

Generosity without moderation is flaunting one's fortune. It's perceived as vulgar, almost obscene. Such gifts are bitterly received, not only because they seem to mean nothing to the donor. They are insults to the receiver.

Worst by far is to rule without modesty. The ruler who wants to be first in the world might cause widespread destruction. Through history, we have had the misfortune of experiencing plenty of them. There are some such rulers today, as well.

We must beware, because those who have the desire to be first in the world will spare no efforts to get there. Once they do, it's extremely difficult and costly to get rid of them. So, we have to consider very carefully what persons we allow to be our leaders.

A golden rule is to avoid giving power to people who want it, or loudly claim to be best fit for it. The best leaders we can find are usually those who are reluctant to shoulder the responsibility. They take it seriously. Those we need to convince to take the job are the ones we should get for it. But those who jump at the opportunity should be stopped at the entrance.

We must learn this. The survival of the world depends on it, now that we have such enormous resources and so terrible weapons at the disposal of our leaders.

Those who remain compassionate, on the other hand, will be successful and avoid blame. Even when they must go to war, if they still remain compassionate they will be victorious and the enemy will not grieve it. That's a mighty power, surpassing most weaponry.

When they defend themselves, remaining compassionate, they will not be conquered, because they have something so fine to protect. The enemy will congratulate them, out of respect for their nobility.

In a sharp conflict, it's necessary to see the adversary as evil and oneself as good. Otherwise it's very difficult to muster up the necessary resolve to fight until winning. The one who remains compassionate is certainly good, and therefore has the most splendid advantage. The enemy will find it hard to hate him.

Even Heaven agrees on this. So, fate seems to work in favor of those who remain compassionate. That's because compassion is a trait of Tao, the Way. The compassionate is treated the same by Tao. Compassion breeds compassion. So, there's no reason to deviate from it.

68

Excellent warriors are not violent.
Excellent soldiers are not furious.
Excellent conquerors do not engage.
Excellent leaders of people lower themselves.

This is called the virtue of no strife.
This is called the use of people's capacity.
This is called the union with Heaven.
It is the perfection of the ancients.

Peaceful Warriors

It would be going too far to state that Lao Tzu is a pacifist. In his book, he seems to admit to the necessity of war in some cases, or the impossibility to avoid it forever. What he does make clear, though, is that even in the case of war there are virtuous actions and non-virtuous ones.

Warriors and warlords may use violence, but they should not be violent. They should not jump to violent solutions. When they find no other way, they should mourn it and be as sparse with the violence as possible. A warrior who revels in violence and brutality is an abomination, also in the eyes of other warriors.

It's not even the most efficient way to wage a war. Violence promotes violent responses, and it makes the enemy increasingly committed to resist the onslaught. When a warlord uses excessive violence, his own troops will be dismayed and the enemy troops will find courage to fight back with tremendous strength and perseverance.

At length, he cannot win.

A furious soldier is inferior in battle. Wrath makes for poor judgment and a dimmed vision. He might be an awe-inspiring sight at first, but when the actual battle commences, he proves to lack many of the abilities necessary to succeed and survive.

It's an inferior and unbalanced state of mind, which may be a misguided way of dealing with the terrible situation, or the consequence of some equally misguided conviction of war being the righteous course of action.

The superior soldiers are the ones who keep being human, in the middle of battle, and continue to cherish peacetime values. That makes them complete also in moments of crisis.

The conqueror eager to engage in battle will soon enough enter one he cannot win. His narrow-minded preference for martial solutions will make him equally narrow-minded in battle. He will be easily outmaneuvered.

His strategy is unrefined and inferior. His perception is clouded. His haste to do battle may catch the enemy by surprise at first, but war is easier to start than to end. His attitude has the tools for the former, but not for the latter.

The superior conqueror waits and tries all other alternatives, before going to war. And when doing so, he is very well prepared. He regrets having to start a war and longs for its ending, so he knows how to reach the latter. If there was any way of succeeding without battle, he would have found it. In many cases there are such alternatives.

Caring Leaders

Lao Tzu moves on to leadership in general, not just on the battlefield. It's the same in every case. Good leaders lower themselves and act humbly in front of the people at their command. Otherwise their leadership will always be questioned, often opposed, and sometimes revolted.

The humble and caring leaders will be met accordingly. Then they can lead with ease.

The leader, who refrains from personal strife, will find people responding by doing their utmost to comply. They are encouraged by a leader who doesn't push a personal agenda, but the common interest. So, they take initiatives to bring their own abilities and make use of them.

If they were displeased with their leader, they would hide their capacities. They would only do what they had to, and do it without commitment. They would be of little use to their leader.

Such leadership, although skilled and wise, would hardly be something as grand as a union with Heaven. Nor is it in accordance with Tao.

Excellent leaders put their own interests aside, work for a common good together with their people, and are reluctant to spring into forceful action. They are indeed following the Way.

69

Warriors say:
I dare not be like the host,
But would rather be like the guest.
I dare not advance an inch,
But would rather retreat a foot.

This is called marching without marching,
Grabbing without arms,
Charging without enemy,
Seizing without weapons.

No misfortune is worse
Than underestimating the enemy.
Underestimating the enemy,
I risk losing my treasure.
Therefore:
When equal armies battle,
The grieving one will be victorious.

Like a Guest

The wise warrior would not invite to battle and presume to control the circumstances. Instead, he considers his actions carefully and expects the unexpected.

He acts like the guest, and not like the host. It's not his party. He is even hesitant about visiting it, and would make other plans if possible.

Therefore he is reluctant to advance even the slightest. He would rather retreat, if that's at all possible. Moving forward is stepping into the unknown, but backwards you return to familiar territory.

Also, the warrior who is eager to advance is the one who nurtures the illusion that war brings good things to the winner. There are no winners in war. Those who know this neither invite to it, nor hurry to advance in it.

The hesitant warrior marches without marching, which is to say that he tries as much as he can to win the war without doing battle. If prepared properly, a war can be won before the battle begins.

To charge without enemy is to arm the country so well in times of peace that war is avoided, or swiftly won. It's arming to avoid war, not to wage it. The same can be said for seizing without weapons.

War Is Failure
Neither the start nor the end of war is decided by what happens in between, but what happens before. War is not the means to an outcome, but an outcome. There was failure to avoid it. Previous conditions and preparations are the decisive factors.

That's why the superior warrior grieves when forced to do battle. To him, it means that something failed, and tragedy for all ensues, no matter who wins and who loses. His grief proves his superiority. Therefore, it's the sign of the winner. Since he regrets going to war he is well prepared to avoid it. That's also the preparation to win it.

Grabbing without arms is an expression that can be compared to using one's arms without rolling up the sleeves. That's how the line is usually translated. When force is used, it should not be announced or displayed.

There is no mistake greater than underestimating the

enemy. That is sure to lead to losing the war. Those who underestimate their enemies are unprepared for them. How could they win? Not only will they lose the war and what they might have sought to gain by it, but their failure is also evidence that they lack essential insight into how the world works.

The greatest of treasures, Tao, is not in their grasp.

The line about the treasure is ambiguous. It could refer only to whatever treasures the warring parties try to defend or seize, but Lao Tzu shifts to First Person. Since Tao is the only thing he really treasures, he indicates that it's lost to a warrior who acts so foolishly.

Indeed, those who hurry to war, thinking that they are sure to win it, have moved very far from the Way. Even if they should be so lucky as to win the war, they have lost something more precious than any land they seize. Soon, also what they conquered will be lost to them, since they lack the wisdom to hold on to it.

War is won by those who know that nothing is won by it.

70

*My words are very easy to understand
And very easy to practice.
Still, no one in the world
Can understand or practice them.*

*My words have an origin.
My deeds have a sovereign.
Truly, because people do not understand this,
They do not understand me.*

*That so few understand me is why I am treasured.
Therefore, the sage wears coarse clothes, concealing jade.*

Easy to Understand

The origin and sovereign of Lao Tzu's words and deeds is obviously one and the same: Tao, the Way. People who don't understand Tao have little chance of understanding what Lao Tzu says, or why he acts the way he does, which is mostly by non-action.

Reading his book, we can understand the difficulty people might have to grasp its content. That difficulty must have been as great in his own time, among his own people. Although they were familiar with the language and the context in which he spoke, his ideas and conclusions must have seemed odd, even mysterious. We still struggle with his words, although science and learning have in some ways taken us closer to his worldview.

So, Lao Tzu remains a treasure.

His text is straightforward. One might even call his words simple. But there's jade inside. The words reveal the treasure of Tao to those who can read them properly. They may be few, even fewer if we just count those who are certain of understanding the text correctly. That would be only those who are already familiar with Tao. Anyone else is not likely to figure it out.

So, we must wonder: For whom was the *Tao Te Ching* written, if those who can understand it already know what it says, and the others are unlikely to learn it by reading the book? Lao Tzu cannot have been very optimistic about the reception of his book. He probably didn't care too much, since he is supposed to have written it when leaving China for good.

He may have written it as a gesture to the ancients, since he thought of them as so much wiser than his contemporaries. A tribute to the wisdom of old.

It's not unique among authors to write for their predecessors instead of the present audience. Maybe they also hope that the future will hold at least a few kindred spirits, appreciating their text properly.

Lao Tzu wrote primarily for his kindred spirits, wherever and whenever they might appear. He probably had not met too many of them in his life.

Lao Tzu as a divinity. Chinese sandstone stele, 515 CE.

道德經

71

Knowing that you do not know is the best.
Not knowing that you do not know is an illness.

Truly, only those who see illness as illness
Can avoid illness.
The sage is not ill,
Because he sees illness as illness.
Therefore he is not ill.

Knowing Illness

Disease awareness and the lack thereof are frequently discussed in relation to mental disease, where the lack of awareness is said to be common. No wonder, since it's the mind that is affected, and it's by the mind one is made aware. One can't see into oneself. Nor is it easy to regard one's actions from an objective perspective, because the mind is subjective by nature.

When Lao Tzu uses the metaphor of illness, he is referring to a mental capacity, but hardly any kind of real insanity. He speaks about the ability to be aware of what you know and what you don't know. They are not easy to tell apart, again a paradox of the mind.

If you know something, that's fine. You know that you know it. But you must also know something to know that you don't know it. Otherwise you can only guess about it.

So, if you know, you can't be completely sure that you really do. If you don't know, it's most likely that you are not aware of it, or you would know at least to some extent.

Maybe the truth lies in the great gray zone between the two extremes, as is so often the case with things in this world.

If you know a little, you may know that it's only a little of it you know. Then you also know that there's more to know, and until you do so, there is a lot you don't know.

Still, we are only concerned with quantities. The quality of knowledge is the extent to which it's true. Every person experiences often through life, how things that one held to be true, later prove to be false. This also goes for society as a whole. What's the truth one day is nothing but nonsense the next day.

Our knowledge keeps increasing, but our knowledge of the truth often changes dramatically. What we take for granted may very well prove to be completely wrong.

The only proper attitude to have towards this is one of modesty and humility. We must keep in mind that knowledge is uncertain and truth is elusive. Then we know that we don't know, and thereby escape the illness.

The uncertainty of knowledge has been discussed by philosophers since ancient times, in the West as well as the East. When Descartes stated that "I think, therefore I am," he pointed out that the only thing I can be sure of is that there is someone wondering – that someone being me. Making sure of anything else is not an easy task. Claiming to be sure of anything else can be quite detrimental.

72

When people do not dread authorities,
Then a greater dread descends.

Do not crowd their dwellings.
Do not make them weary at their work.
If you do not make them weary,
They will not be weary of you.

Therefore, the sage knows himself,
But does not parade.
He cherishes himself,
But does not praise himself.
He discards the one,
And chooses the other.

Don't Make Them Weary

The second part of the *Tao Te Ching* has several chapters on government, and how to improve it. This is one of them. What Lao Tzu expresses in his views on governing the country, often seems very similar to modern democratic ideals. That would be going too far, though.

It's clear that he thinks of a state ruled by a sovereign who doesn't need regular voting procedures to stay in power, or a parliament to convince. He thinks of kings and dukes and the like. Their power is not questioned, but their use of it is.

Lao Tzu doesn't hope for a revolution. He might even abhor it, if he were able to imagine such a thing. He thinks about the existing authorities, and what advice he would give them.

Legend has it that he did himself work as a government official, although not a very prominent one, before leaving the country in dismay. So, he knew about the shortcomings of leadership, and the damages it brought to the empire as well as its population. When writing a text of as much as five thousand words, he was bound to touch on the subject.

Apart from insisting on the ruler's responsibility to act according to Tao, the Way, Lao Tzu also stresses again and again that the ruler should work for the best of the people. That was by no means the norm in his time. In many countries around the world it still isn't.

The emperor had the whole country at his disposal, to do whatever he wanted with it, as if his wishes came from Heaven. Concern for the people was far down on the list.

Lao Tzu brings it up to first place, and he has two main reasons for it. One is that compassion and careful concern are in accordance with Tao. With such leadership the country would progress as it should, to everyone's delight.

The other reason is that a ruler who ignores the needs and sentiments of his subjects may be overthrown. To Lao Tzu, a rebellion of that kind, no matter how understandable, deviates even more from the Way than bad leadership does. In his mind, it would open for chaos.

The world is governed by Tao, and a country should be governed by a king. Lao Tzu sees no alternative. But the king needs to follow Tao, or the whole order is at risk.

In this chapter he points out that a ruler should execute his powers mildly. If people are too burdened by their ruler, they will cease to respect him, and obey him as little as they can get away with.

If he inflicts on their homes, narrowing their space of living, he strikes them where it really hurts. There will be a reaction. The same is likely if he harasses them at their work, demanding too much or disturbing them in their daily chores. They can't let that continue at length, or they risk their very livelihood.

A ruler is free to do a lot of things and take heavy tolls from his subjects. But if he shakes the very ground under their feet, they must counter it somehow.

Lao Tzu expresses it by playing with words, using 'weary' in ambiguous ways, but the subject is quite serious. The ruler needs the people's trust, and that can only be reached by proving worthy of it.

The sage trusts his own capacity and wisdom, but still remains humble and discreet. So should a ruler. It's the best way to serve Heaven and Tao, but it can only be done by primarily serving the people.

73

Those who have the courage to dare will perish.
Those who have the courage not to dare will live.
Of those two, one is beneficial and one is harmful.
What Heaven detests, who knows why?
Even the sage considers it difficult.

Heaven's Way does not contend,
Yet it certainly triumphs.
It does not speak,
Yet it certainly answers.
It does not summon,
Yet things come by themselves.
It seems to be at rest,
Yet it certainly has a plan.

Heaven's net is very vast.
It is sparsely meshed, yet nothing slips through.

Heaven's Way

Heaven's Way, *T'ien chih Tao*, is a concept that was old and established already at the time of Lao Tzu. Mankind has always observed and awed at the many movements in the sky. Clouds of different shades and shapes sail through it, occasional rain or snow falls from it, the sun and moon travel it in fixed cycles, and the stars appear in millions at clear skied nights.

It's a marvel, indeed, with significant importance to earthly life.

Heaven has been studied for at least as long as we have historical records of human thought, probably much longer than that. People searched to explain these events and to foresee them. Although the sky was way out of reach, or maybe just because of this, mankind feared it and struggled to understand its dynamics. Astrology is just one of those efforts.

The search for the way in which the sky behaves is what once formed the concept of Heaven's Way.

In Chinese tradition, and many others around the world, Heaven was regarded as the ruling force of the whole world, shaping everything else to conform to its ways.

This power of Heaven was not necessarily seen as belonging to some kind of divinity. It could be described as divine in itself, but just as impersonal as the Tao of which Lao Tzu speaks. It was regarded as a sovereign power, indeed, but more of a natural law than an entity with its own thoughts and wishes.

That's why even the sage has problems understanding some of its traits. Why would a natural law have preferences that seem to be moral ones? Still, when Lao Tzu observes the world around him, he comes to the conclusion that Heaven's Way clearly prefers some directions, and avoids other ones as if with disgust.

He draws the conclusion that the laws of Tao are for the best, not because they benefit the most, although they do, but just because the laws of Tao have formed the world.

One could say that the laws of Tao are for the best, simply because there is nothing else.

The expression Heaven's Way in this chapter is most likely to stand for Tao, the Way. It's cause for thought that Lao Tzu would use this expression instead of just calling it

Tao, as usual. This appears in the chapters 9, 47, 73, 77, 79, and 81. There might be an influence from other sources involved, maybe an addition in a later copy of the text.

In other Chinese traditions, Heaven's Way was supreme to any other Way. In Lao Tzu's universe, Tao is the first cause and the master of all. Already in the first chapter, he has established that Tao is the beginning of Heaven and Earth, so Heaven's Way must be something later and inferior.

Therefore, I would not be surprised if future findings of older manuscripts show that Heaven is a later addition to this chapter, or the whole chapter might be a later construction.

The oldest manuscript of the *Tao Te Ching* found so far is that from Guodian, which dates back to around 300 BC. There, none of the chapters 67 to 81 can be found. The manuscript is far from complete, so nothing is certain, but the absence of this big chunk of the text suggests later additions. That would also explain why many of the thoughts in the *Tao Te Ching* are repeated in several chapters of its present form.

On the other hand, it might simply mean that this chunk somehow got lost from the rest of the Guodian manuscript.

Chapter 9, which also uses the expression Heaven's Way, is included in the Guodian manuscript, and so is this expression at the proper place. The other chapters where the expression occurs are absent from the Guodian manuscript.

We need additional findings to make any solid conclusions about the matter. Still, in the following I assume that Heaven and its Way in this chapter is synonymous to Tao.

Courage

The chapter begins with an observation to which we can all easily relate. The daring ones who jump into danger are likely to meet with disaster.

Refusing those dares is another kind of courage, which might be despised by some. It's not an inferior kind of courage, but it reduces the risk of harm.

Strangely, society seems to praise the attitude that seeks danger, as if welcoming disaster. It's as if society as a whole, similar to many of its members, nourishes some kind of death wish.

In traditional Christianity, suicide was a serious sin. Such corpses were buried outside the cemeteries, and in his *Divine Comedy*, Dante placed them in the very worst part of Hell. Suicide was despised because it was seen as throwing away the gift from God, who was the source of all life. Committing suicide was ungrateful. Also, it was a kind of sabotage of God's plan, which applied to each and every living creature.

Tao's disapproval of people risking their lives may be something similar. It goes against the plan, the pattern and direction constituting the Way. People should try to stay alive, as a way of conforming to their nature.

The more we cling to life, the less we are inclined to act irresponsibly and put ourselves at risk. The world would be a much more peaceful place if we learned this. Some would say boring, but that remains to be seen.

Tao Is Hiding

What triumphs without contending, answers without speaking, attracts without summoning, and pursues a plan although resting, is definitely Tao, the Way. It's the hidden ruler, the truth written on everything in the world, the center of all, and the process that everything adapts to by itself.

It's the Way nature is.

Its structure covers all, but not tightly like the peel encloses the orange. Tao is hiding in the background and in the minute. It's better described as a net connecting all things in the world, but still allowing them to move rather freely. Its meshes are so sparse that it seems to consist only of holes, but nothing escapes it, since it's the fabric of which the universe is made.

74

If people are not afraid of dying,
Why threaten them with death?
If people live in constant fear of death,
And if breaking the law is punished by death,
Then who would dare?

There is one appointed supreme executioner.
Truly, trying to take the place of the supreme executioner
Is like trying to carve wood like a master carpenter.
Of those who try to carve wood like a master carpenter,
There are few who do not injure their hands.

The Supreme Executioner

This chapter is unclear in several ways, in its Chinese original, and has been translated in quite different manners. The first part deals with the fear of death, the second with the executioner. The subjects connect, since Lao Tzu first discusses how fear of the death penalty makes people abide by the law, and then moves on to the one executing the punishment.

The complication lies in precisely what he has to say about these things.

In the first part, it's possible to read the second question as who dares to be an executioner, instead of who dares to break the law. That doesn't make much sense, if the fear of death is not supposed to be the fear of inducing it, as well as being struck by it.

A fear of being the executioner is probably not what Lao

Tzu implies, since it has nothing to do with the fear of breaking the law. The executioner acts to uphold the law, not to break it. So, I translate this part to deal with the fear of dying. Lao Tzu has commented this also in other chapters.

That makes the message of the first part of the chapter quite obvious: people obey the laws if they fear the punishment. They obey them completely if they risk capital punishment.

This can be discussed. The death penalty exists in many countries, but crimes are still committed there. Lao Tzu would conclude that some people in those countries don't fear death, at least not enough to refrain from criminality.

It's hard to argue with such a statement, since it's very difficult to falsify. How to prove that people don't fear death enough? Actually, if they risk getting killed, they are obviously not overcome by the fear of it.

As Lao Tzu says, they would need to be in constant fear of death. Otherwise they might at times be forgetful of it, and at such times they would be tempted to commit the crimes that the death penalty was supposed to prevent. This fear would only work if it were an obsession.

The chapter has been interpreted as Lao Tzu's support for the death penalty. I doubt it. Here, he really says that it demands total obsession with this fear, which would be a terrible life. In the following chapter he will continue his reasoning by explaining why people are not that fearful of death.

Instead of advocating the death penalty, he may be pointing out its shortcomings and hinting at solutions elsewhere.

Nature Kills

That would explain the next part of this chapter, where he moves on to say that there is one supreme executioner, who cannot be imitated without risk. That master executioner is nature. Death from natural causes is the unavoidable executioner who never fails. Why should we try to compete with it?

Nature behaves according to Tao, so this must be true for natural causes as well. The supreme executioner is appointed by none other than Tao, that is to say it's in accordance with the Way, and part of its structure. If we try to take it upon ourselves to decide when people should live and when they should die, then we surely deviate from the Way. That is bound to fail.

An alternative interpretation of this part of the chapter makes the supreme executioner the human being appointed by the government. That would make some vague sense if the first part of the chapter asks who dares to execute others, but the train of thought would still be odd.

If we are afraid of killing, then we hardly aim to take the role of the executioner. So, in this case the second part of the chapter is meaninglessly just stating what we already know and support. That's not very likely.

We can't apply our present questioning of the capital punishment on something written more than two thousand years ago. In the society where Lao Tzu lived, there was little ethical opposition to the death penalty.

But Lao Tzu's Tao is one where any action should be considered carefully, and avoided if at all possible. Putting people to death would be drastic also in the eyes of the people at his time, so it would be strange if he didn't feel uncomfortable with it.

Also, he states repeatedly that violent solutions are the worst.

It's not unthinkable that Lao Tzu wished to argue against the death penalty, as well as other forceful actions common in his time – as in ours. If so, the first part of this chapter presents a common argument for the death penalty. It's supposed to work as a deterrent. But then the second part starts to explain why this is not a valid excuse.

In the next chapter he continues by stating that people aren't that afraid of death, because of society's imperfection. So, the deterrent doesn't work. Then there is no good reason for the killing.

Society should be protective of its people, like a mother, and not brutal like a vindictive warrior. Lao Tzu might not insist on an end to the death penalty, but he is not likely to believe that it benefits society.

75

People starve.
The rulers consume too much with their taxes.
That is why people starve.

People are hard to govern.
The rulers interfere with too much.
That is why people are hard to govern.

People take death lightly.
They expect too much of life.
That is why people take death lightly.

Truly, only acting without thought of one's life
Is superior to valuing one's life.

People versus Rulers

There are people and there are rulers. Their relation is a complicated one, to say the least. People often have great difficulties suffering the demands of the rulers, and the rulers can have great problems making people obey their commands. Lao Tzu gives some hints to why this is so.

He blames the rulers, because they have the responsibility and the power to make changes. Common people usually don't.

High taxes were a problem then, as they are now. Governments are insatiable. Taxes are their means, without which they would not be able to do anything.

Power is money and money is power. Those who have

the one get the other, and the more they have, the more they can get.

Suddenly, they get too much, and people starve. In the case of ancient China, some taxes could very well be in rice, so over-consumption at one end led directly to starvation at the other end. But the effect is the same when the tax is paid in the form of money.

Sadly, governments are tempted to take all but exactly what people need to survive, and sometimes they do it so narrowly that this crucial limit is exceeded. The excuses vary through time, but the greed is the same.

Of course, people who are pushed to starvation will be difficult to govern, but this can happen for many other reasons. The common denominator is exaggerated interference, which can be said about excess taxation, too.

When governments interfere too much with the lives of the people, there are bound to be reactions, protests, and a general unwillingness to comply. People can cause problems for their leaders in so many ways, only some of them obvious enough to counteract. When pressured, they will swiftly find all these possibilities.

Insufficient Fear

In the former chapter, Lao Tzu talked about threatening people with the death penalty, to make them obedient, and how complicated that can be. He returns to the subject here, explaining why people are not so afraid of dying.

They expect too much of life, which means that they hurry to experience this or that sensation, not bothering to consider risks that may be involved. Their appetite for life is so big that they become forgetful of hazards, and have no time for reflection.

It's like children playing wildly, forgetting to consider their own safety. When we are drunk on life, we feel invulnerable, and like the young we believe death to be as far off as if we were immortal.

If we don't get as much out of life as we wished, then it loses its charm. That way, too, we cease to fear death, even if we don't exactly want it at the very next moment. Expecting too much of life must lead to disappointment. Death loses its horror to the extent that life loses its charm.

To the same extent, the rulers lose their power over us, since they no longer have the ultimate threat at their disposal. Any other threat would also lose its bite, when we don't shudder at the thought of being killed. It brings a kind of freedom to the people, but in a risky fashion.

Lao Tzu recommends that we take life seriously and hold on to it. That's in accordance with our nature. We should do our best to survive as long as possible. But he doesn't regard it as the most ideal relation to life.

One attitude surpasses it. That's to act without being concerned about one's own survival, which is utter unselfishness. For the greatest good, we should be able to sacrifice ourselves without hesitation. Also, we should willingly risk our lives to help avoid the greatest evil.

So, we should strive to stay alive as long as that can be done without deviating from Tao, the Way. But we should follow the Way without worrying about how we personally might suffer along it. Lao Tzu assures us that no harm comes to us if we follow Tao, but to do so we must dare risking even our lives.

In other words, to live life properly, we can't be obsessed by the fear of death.

76

People are born soft and weak.
They die hard and stiff.
All things such as grass and trees
Are soft and supple in life.
At their death they are withered and dry.

So, the hard and stiff are death's companions.
The soft and weak are life's companions.

Therefore:
The unyielding army will not win.
The rigid tree will be felled.
The rigid and big belong below.
The soft and weak belong above.

Life Is Soft and Weak

Lao Tzu uses drastic imagery, comparing the newborn baby with the dead corpse, the former being soft and the latter stiffening in *rigor mortis*. The fact that we stiffen after death confirms the point he wants to make.

Life is characterized by supple softness, growth, and the ability to adapt. Death is rigid, and the only change coming is that into dust.

The world certainly shows with all possible clarity what we should be in life, and what leads to death.

These self-evident conditions to life can be applied to so much within it. In war, the army that can move and adapt is most likely to win the war. Trees that harden and start to dry up inside will be felled by wind or by ax. If not, they finally fall by themselves.

The rigid, no matter how proudly it rose above everything else, will tumble. The soft and yielding, no matter how small it was in the beginning, will move upwards in its continued adaption, until it rises above all. As long as it keeps its supple vitality, it will grow and advance.

That goes for living beings as well as for their ventures.

It's true on so many levels. The biggest company in the world will soon go bankrupt if it doesn't adapt to changes in its line of business. The greatest nation will perish if it refuses to recognize changes inside or outside its borders. A leader who can't compromise will soon lose his power. An expert who rejects new discoveries descends into ignorance. A person who ceases to be curious grows tired and loses the lust for life.

We live as long as we adapt to life, which always changes. We start dying at the moment we begin to oppose that fundamental fact of life. There's the essence of longevity.

77

Heaven's Way is like stretching a bow.
The high is lowered and the low is raised.
Excess is reduced and deficiency is replenished.

Heaven's Way reduces excess and replenishes deficiency.
People's Way is not so.
They reduce the deficient and supply the excessive.
Who has excess and supplies the world?
Only the one who follows the Way.

Therefore, the sage acts without taking credit.
He accomplishes without dwelling on it.
He does not want to display his worth.

Raise the Low

Here, Lao Tzu again uses the expression Heaven's Way as if it's synonymous with Tao, the Way. It's a bit strange that he would do so, considering his otherwise consistent perspective on Tao preceding everything, including Heaven. To Lao Tzu, Tao is superior to all. Accordingly, Heaven's Way must be something lesser and later than the Way itself. I discuss this at chapter 73, where it also appears.

Anyway, what this chapter speaks of is hardly dependent on the definition of Heaven's Way.

Lao Tzu points out that the natural order of things is that excess should be reduced and deficiency should be replenished.

That's what water does by itself, and we are told that

water behaves like Tao. It moves downwards, striving to balance high and low to a perfect middle.

Our society is certainly different. That's just as true today as it was in ancient China. The rich get richer and the poor get poorer. Wealth tends to move from those who don't have enough to those who have more than enough. It's true on the individual level, as well as for nations. Also, there are big differences of wealth between whole continents.

It's a tragedy that seems to have no end.

The sage refuses to participate in this deplorable process. Not only does he avoid getting what he doesn't need, but he also escapes being praised above others, although he might deserve it. He completes his tasks without expecting any reward. When he is done he just moves on.

Otherwise, society would surely hurry to make him one of the privileged, and cover him with gold.

Some have to struggle not to get more than they need, others don't get what they need no matter how they struggle. What's really needed, is that those who have more than they need give it to all those in the world who need it. Unfortunately, that's a struggle that few of the wealthy are willing to undertake.

78

Nothing in the world is softer and weaker than water.
Yet, to attack the hard and strong,
Nothing surpasses it.
Nothing can take its place.

The weak overcomes the strong.
The soft overcomes the hard.
Everybody in the world knows this,
Still nobody makes use of it.

Therefore the sage says:
To bear the country's disgrace
Is to rule the shrines of soil and grain.
To bear the country's misfortunes
Is to be the king of the world.

True words seem false.

Water Surpasses All

Lao Tzu returns to what must be his favorite metaphor for the primary quality of Tao, the Way. Water is yielding, which is exactly what makes it superior. As the Roman poet Ovid pointed out: Dripping water hollows out the stone, not through force but through persistence.

Water embraces instead of confronts, it caresses instead of beats, but it still subdues, eventually.

Of course, water can sometimes be a mighty striking force, but Lao Tzu refers to its yielding quality and its nature to seek the lowest place. That's what he admires in it, and that's what he wants us to learn, in just about everything we do.

Not only water is soft and weak in its behavior towards its surroundings, and still overcomes resistance. Many things in nature show the same traits and get the same results. The air even surpasses water in softness and weakness, but it tends to travel upwards, aiming for the sky. Otherwise it would surely become Lao Tzu's ideal example.

Anyway, nature tells us repeatedly to trust the soft and the weak, but we don't learn. As soon as we are eager to accomplish something, we go for the hard and strong. We lack the persistence that Ovid mentioned.

Persistence is a recurring theme in another Chinese classic, *I Ching*, the Book of Change. It states several times that persistence in a righteous course brings reward.

Ancient China was a country cherishing tradition and values of old, so the patience to persist was highly appreciated and recommended. We may not have the same ideal today, it seems.

Yielding

Lao Tzu doesn't state that persistence is the essence of what he advocates. Instead, he points out the yielding. If we can accept instead of oppose, and let go instead of confront, we can accomplish anything.

There are few obstacles that need to be destroyed. Most of them can simply be circumvented. Often when we choose the path of confrontation, we do so because of irrelevant factors, such as our pride and our impatience. Although we regard ourselves as the reasoning species, *Homo sapiens*, many of our actions are induced by our bad temper.

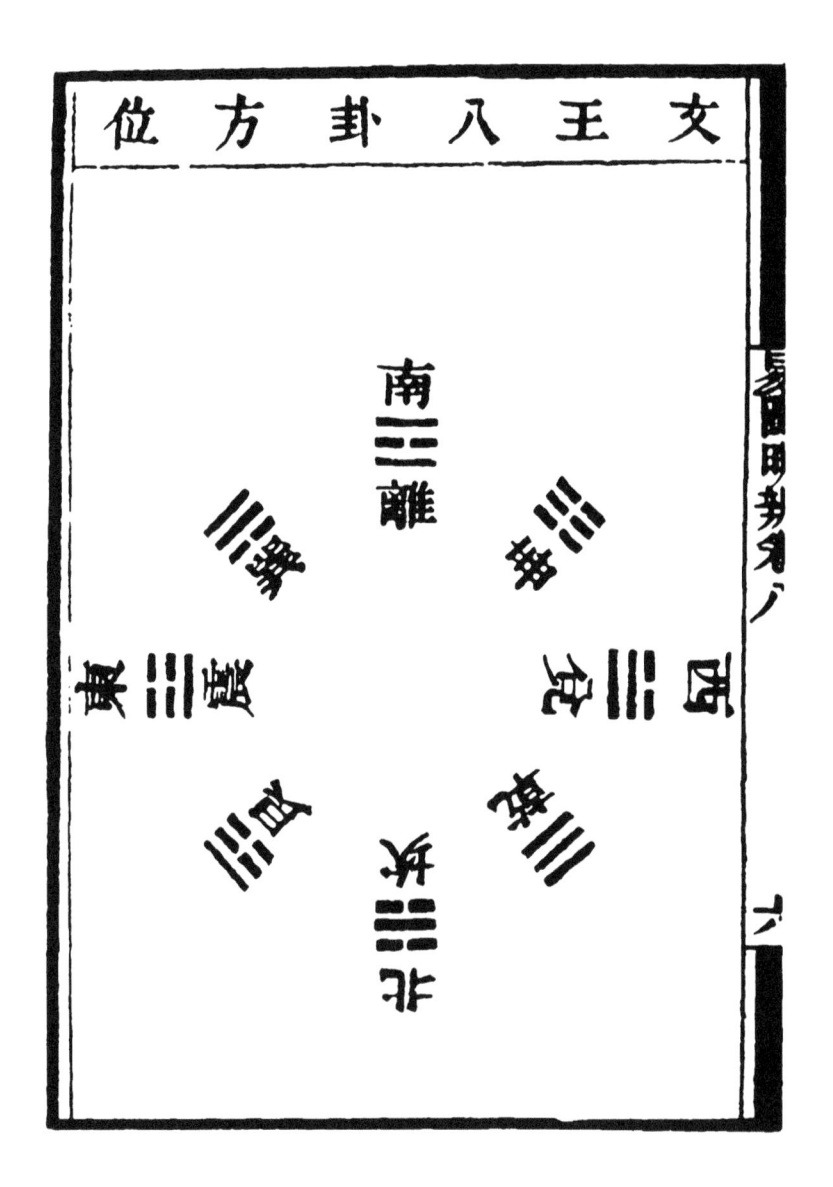

Pa kua, the eight trigrams, based on the polarity of yin and yang. The trigrams are the essentials of I Ching, the Book of Change. There, they are combined into 64 different hexagrams, which are used for divination. Illustration by Hu Wei, 1706.

道德經

We would all gain by yielding and humbling ourselves. Thereby we would overcome our pride, which feeds our temper, which triggers our impatience. This is even more necessary in a ruler. So, the sage begins by lowering himself and accepting the suffering that may be inevitable.

He expects disgrace rather than praise, which is why he is apt to rule the old shrines of offerings to soil and grain. Those were places for important agricultural rituals in ancient China, so their ruler would be the ruler of the whole country.

The sage is also willing to share the misfortunes of the country, instead of using his power to isolate himself from them. That makes him fit to rule the whole world.

There are far too many rulers who use their power first and foremost to get personal benefits, and who blame everyone and everything for what might go wrong. That's just as true now as it was in the time of Lao Tzu.

He knew in what way they needed to change, but it seems neither he nor we have found out how to make them go through with that change. Nor have we learned how to avoid such rulers getting into power. Our problem might be that people who would as rulers live up to Lao Tzu's ideal are so rare.

79

When bitter enemies make peace,
Surely some bitterness remains.
How can this be solved?

Therefore:
The sage honors his part of the settlement,
But does not exact his due from others.
The virtuous carry out the settlement,
But those without virtue pursue their claims.

Heaven's Way gives no favors.
It always remains with good people.

Honor the Settlement

William Shakespeare dedicated one of his greatest dramas, *Romeo and Juliet*, to the tragic fact that conflict is so hard to end. Two families remain in a feud that has lasted for generations. It doesn't end until the highest price is paid for it – the death of both Romeo and his Juliet.

It's a human tragedy, indeed, that animosity is so easily started and so painstaking to stop. Once aggression has been expressed and returned, bitterness lingers on, whatever conclusion is reached. It can remain for hundreds of years, through many generations, even when the original cause for it is forgotten. New reasons will be invented on the way. When bitterness remains, the animosity is renewed and enforced even by the most ridiculous little mishap.

Making true and lasting peace between two enemies of

old is as delicate a process as walking on thin ice. The same is true for a conflict that has escalated to severe violence. So many human shortcomings are involved, such as our pride, our temper, and our distrust in each other.

Fear might be the key ingredient here, as in so many other human failures. We dare do nothing else but prepare for the worst we suspect from our adversaries, and that's usually by doing it first. Disaster is bound to follow.

Again, yielding is the only way out. If we have the courage and the unselfishness to begin by sacrifices of our own, then our enemy can begin to relax. Peace is not accomplished with swords drawn, and only by sheathing our own swords can we expect our enemies to do the same.

Peace is worth the risk.

Among historians, it's strongly believed that one of the important reasons for the outbreak of World War II was the treaty after World War I. The victorious states demanded great sacrifices from Germany after the first war, so bitterness remained and continued to grow, making it much easier for Hitler to throw Germany into the second war.

The world community learned its lesson, as did the families Montague and Capulet after the death of their children. After World War II, the conquered nations were treated with some care and concern. They were completely disarmed, but that worked to their own economic advantage. No punishments were issued, except for some German leaders in the Nuremberg trials, which came very close to complete failure.

Nothing good comes out of striking at those who have already surrendered. Violent conflict is a tragedy. When it's ended, we should all concentrate on comforting and healing each other. Otherwise, it just has not ended.

Two Winners

Lao Tzu widens this to apply for any kind of settlement or agreement. The sage will concentrate on living up to his promise, whereas a lesser person is fixed on making sure that he gets his share, but ignores what he had agreed to contribute.

If both behave like the latter, then an escalating conflict is hard to avoid. But if one begins by showing trust and paying what he is due, then at length it will be very difficult for the other not to do the same.

Even if the reluctant party doesn't contribute, it's better to let it go than to insist on his fulfillment of the settlement. There are not many things a settlement can contain, which are worth an escalated conflict with little hope of a peaceful solution. Certainly not if war might follow.

Usually, when one of the parties is very reluctant to hold to his part, the settlement was unfair to begin with. A contract of any kind should have two winners. Otherwise, at least one of them is a loser. That party will become bitter and refuse.

Even if the loser accepts and delivers, bitterness will follow. And bitterness is such that it remains for very long, if not dealt with properly.

A contract, as fair as the judgment of King Salomon, creates problems if one of the parties still feels disadvantaged. Whether this feeling is legitimate or not, bitterness is born.

In a good solution, both parties not only benefit equally, but are convinced of it. The next best solution is if the party that can live with it the easiest, volunteers to gain the least from the settlement. An agreement is a delicate matter. It should be built on giving, not on taking.

Heaven's Way, which must again be a synonym for Tao,

the Way, allows no favors. In each situation, it is present where the virtuous one goes, and where the most virtuous decision leads. It's not so that it favors the virtuous. It is present where the virtuous go, because they follow the Way.

Tao makes no adjustment for anybody. It twists and turns for nobody. It needs to be followed to be present. Therefore, those who follow it will benefit.

The Taoist Good

The good that Lao Tzu refers to here, should not be confused with the Christian idea of being good. There are great similarities, but also differences.

For example, to be a good Christian means to act with compassion towards fellow men, for their sake. The good Taoist, on the other hand, treats other people with compassion, but it's as a result of following the Way, the grand plan of the universe. It's not for the sake of other people, but because it's the best line of action for the whole world.

That sometimes means people can be sacrificed, as mentioned in chapter 5, for the good of the whole. In some situations it's necessary to treat people as mere offerings. The Christian idea is practically the opposite. Everything else should be sacrificed for the good of the people. Well, everything but people's own willingness to make sacrifices for the good of other people. An interesting paradox.

The good used by Lao Tzu, *shan*, refers to the virtuous, righteous, charitable, and kind. It points to actions that are beneficial and in accordance with Heaven's order.

Lao Tzu would probably say that the only completely good is to follow Tao completely. Those who do are good, and so are their actions, as a consequence of following the Way. What they are and what they do lead to Tao.

80

Let the country be small,
And the inhabitants few.

Although there are weapons
For tens and hundreds of soldiers,
They will not be used.
Let people take death seriously,
And not travel far.
Although they have boats and carriages,
There's no occasion to use them.
Although they have armor and weapons,
There's no occasion to wear them.
Let people return to making knots on ropes,
Instead of writing.

Their food will be tasty.
Their clothes will be comfortable.
Their homes will be tranquil.
They will rejoice in their daily life.

They can see their neighbors.
Roosters and dogs can be heard from there.
Still, they will age and die
Without visiting one another.

Simple Utopia

Making knots on ropes was believed to be a forerunner to the sophisticated Chinese pictogram writing. Lao Tzu expresses a longing back to previous times, when things were simpler.

I have some problems with this chapter. It describes what Lao Tzu regards as a dream society, but I find it kind of boring. No travel, no visions, no aspirations, and no curiosity. Nothing but the routine of everyday life. It's certainly peaceful and secure, but isn't it also dull?

Not to Lao Tzu, evidently. He praises this life, which could be described with his favorite image of the uncarved wood. We would call it rustic.

People have boats and carriages, but no longing to use them for exploring other parts of the world. They see the neighboring village and hear sounds from there, but don't bother walking the short distance to visit and get to know its inhabitants.

What kind of life is that? What kind of peace and security? To me, it seems like sleep, and a dreamless one at that.

Prison or Sanctuary

Lao Tzu is tired of the spectacular and the grand. He longs back to the basic qualities of life. That's possible for someone who has experienced the world, and gotten enough of it. For those who are yet to explore it, the simple village life might be closer to a prison than a sanctuary.

Of course, what he describes has a lasting charm. No war. No frustrated longing for a greener pasture elsewhere. People are content with what they have, so they know how to enjoy it fully.

The food they make may be simple, but it's tasty and filling. Their clothes may be colorless and coarse, without any fancy decorations, but they are comfortable and therefore pretty, too. Their homes are no palaces, but they find security in them. A house doesn't need to be big to be a home.

People who enjoy the simple everyday life are free from anguished longings for what very few can get. They will not be tempted by things they can't reach, and they will not suffer because they have less luxury than the emperor, his dukes and generals. Only by not longing for something else, you can truly enjoy what you have.

Many people have this ability. There is reason to envy them. If we are pleased with a life of simplicity, nothing can surpass it. Still, I'm not sure I would be satisfied.

I also doubt that Lao Tzu, that splendid mind pondering the hidden workings of the universe, would have settled for it, if he didn't first go out into the world to explore and understand it.

What he describes is not a perfect life for everyone, but a perfect retirement plan. The human being is not able to settle for steady peace and quiet, until after having experienced at least one adventure.

81

True words are not pleasing.
Pleasing words are not true.
Those who are right do not argue.
Those who argue are not right.
Those who know are not learned.
Those who are learned do not know.

The sage does not hoard.
The more he does for others,
The more he has.
The more he thereby gives to others,
The ever more he gets.

Heaven's Way
Is to benefit and not to harm.
The sage's Way
Is to act and not to contend.

The Ideal

The final chapter of the *Tao Te Ching* sums up the most important aspects of living up to the ideal of Tao, the Way, and what signifies the sage who follows it. The similarities to the Christian ideals, as expressed in the words of Jesus, are obvious. This whole chapter could be summarized: "Do unto others as you would have them do unto you."

This proximity to Christian ethics would raise hesitation, since we have the tendency to interpret foreign cultures and thoughts according to our own beliefs. Could we be reading things into Lao Tzu that come from our own minds and not his?

But this golden rule is far from unique to Christianity. It can be found in numerous other traditions and philosophies. It's not unlikely for Lao Tzu to share it. Also, the *Tao Te Ching* contains many similar thoughts, as well as several arguments that lead to the same conclusion.

The unselfish ideal is universal. Lao Tzu clearly supports it, too.

One should not spend life gathering riches and privileges that others lack, although they might need them more. One should try to do good without forcing it upon people, and without needing to take credit for it. We should all try to help and care for one another. It's as simple as that.

If we could, we would swiftly reach Heaven on Earth.

Words, Words, Words
Also in his warnings against false speech and preaching, Lao Tzu expresses thoughts very close to those of Jesus and other thinkers through time. The truth is not always pleasant to hear. Those, whose words are always pleasing, probably avoid words that would upset us, whether they are true or not.

There's a lot of that going on, nowadays. Flattery, hypocrisy, and empty promises are poured over us constantly. The truth is said to be relative, which is taken as an excuse for bending it to one's liking and advantage.

It's also far too common for people in positions of responsibility to hide their failures and shortcomings by not telling us what they know. And in our everyday life we claim to be kind, by serving each other numerous white lies and flattery, but rarely sincerity.

This use of words has gone on so long and so much, that we are ourselves confused about whether or not what we say is true. We lie so much that we get lost in it, and we say so much that we can't keep track of it. As Hamlet says: "Words, words, words." We need to halt the flow and examine its content, before continuing.

Arguments can be constructive when those involved use them to investigate their thoughts, striving for conclusions that all can agree upon. But there are lots of arguments where that process doesn't take place, and they are usually the most heated ones, going on the longest. Sadly, they are also usually about the most important topics.

We listen the least when we talk the loudest. Many arguments are not exchanges of views, but repeated statements of the refusal to discuss.

Those who are right and know it, don't feel protective about it. Mistakes and lies are short-lived, but the truth will most certainly prevail without battle. It's what remains when lies have been revealed and mistakes have been corrected.

Truth wins without a fight, so there's no need to start one over it. The only thing needed is some patience. If we impatiently insist on the truth, we will be less convincing and it will just take longer for the truth to win.

When truth is fought for, it seems to be untrue. Why else fight for it? Countless times, we have experienced how lies and deceptions were forced on us, so we have good reason to suspect whatever is aggressively propagated.

The sage just lowers his voice and waits for sincere questions. They will come.

Wisdom, Not Learning

There is much good to say about learning, but it doesn't necessarily bring wisdom. Knowing the facts is not the same as understanding what they represent or prove. Good learning is gathered in order to have substantial material for reaching conclusions. But learning without concluding is as meaningless as amassing riches that one cannot ever spend in a lifetime. It's excessive baggage.

Our time is one of rapidly growing knowledge. The total of human knowledge is said to be doubled every few years. But most of this knowledge is in need of processing. It has yet to be used for conclusions. We number things and name them, but that's not to understand them. We're just expanding our catalogs.

Sadly, this rapidly increased knowledge and the widening gap to our understanding of it, leave most people in bewilderment. Not only is there more and more we have no chance of getting to know, but we also gasp at all we need to learn in order to introduce ourselves to any specific subject. Reaching knowledge about even the smallest thing seems like a gargantuan feat.

So, the more human knowledge is gathered, the less we know and the farther we get from understanding. There is less and less that we dare to believe we comprehend, without being experts on it.

That way, our society is quickly moving towards a world ruled by experts, as if there are always facts demanding this or that solution, and neither priorities nor ideals have anything to do with it. As if society is merely a machine and we are its fuel.

But facts are often inconclusive and experts are rarely infallible. Any social situation is so complex that several options are present. When we make our choices, we need to consider what future we want to reach.

We cannot surrender our responsibilities to facts that are yet uncertain or ambiguous. Nor can we allow those who claim to be the most learned to make all our choices for us. That ends in a world nobody wanted.

Knowledge without true understanding is blind. If we follow the blind we are sure to leave the Way.

Tao, the Way, is to benefit and not to harm. Therefore we know that what doesn't benefit us is not according to Tao, and it will probably harm us. A simple rule. When we are considering what path to follow and how to act, we can simply choose what's the most beneficial and the least harmful.

All through our history, we have far too many examples of this simple rule being neglected, and the costly results thereof.

It's not easy to follow Tao, the Way, but the result is certainly worth the effort.

Ching

經

Literature

Wang Pi	Mawangdui A	Mawangdui B
道可道	道可道也╱	道可道也
非常道	非恆道也╱	□□□
名可名	名可名也·	□□□
非常名	非恆名也	□恆名也
無名天地之始	無名萬物之始也╱	無名萬物之始也
有名萬物之母	有名萬物之母也□	有名萬物之母也
故常無欲以觀其妙	恆無欲也以觀其眇╱	故恆無欲也□□□
常有欲以觀其徼	恆有欲也以觀其所噭	恆又欲也以觀·所
此兩者同出而異名	兩者同出異名	噭兩者同出異名
同謂之玄	同胃玄	同胃玄
玄之又玄	之有玄	之又玄
眾妙之門	眾眇之□	眾眇之門

Three versions of the first chapter. Squares mark damaged parts of the text. The chapter is missing in the Guodian manuscript.
The ching sign on the previous page is a calligraphy by the author.

Literature

There's a forest of books about Taoism, Lao Tzu, and the *Tao Te Ching*. It makes no sense to list them all, so I have chosen a few versions of the *Tao Te Ching* that I value or find significant in the continued exploration of Lao Tzu's thoughts. Less important works are also included, if they appeared before the present flood of Taoism texts emerged.

The subject is a hot one, so new books will appear as you read this, but I believe that some of the sources listed below will not that quickly be obsolete.

I have added a short comment to every version listed. It's just my personal opinion, so don't trust it any longer than you find it useful. Once you have started your own exploration of the subject, there's no guide more trustworthy than your own inkling.

As for the resources on the Internet, they change so quickly that I can only recommend a Google search (or whatever search engine is the most prominent one, when you read this). Notice that different spellings give partly different search results. For example, *Tao Te Ching*, *Dao De Jing*, and *Daodejing* searches differ, although the major search engines regard them as synonymous. The same is true for *Lao Tzu*, *Lao Zi*, and *Laozi*. Many complete translations of the *Tao Te Ching* are available on the Internet.

Tao Te Ching Versions

Ames, Roger T. & Hall, David L.: DAO DE JING
New York, Ballantine 2003.
A knowledgeable and rather daring version, which also presents the text in Chinese. The findings in Guodian are richly presented and included in the interpretation.

Blakney, Raymond B.: LAO TZU
USA, New American Library 1955.
A straightforward and clear version of the text, with elaborate comments and explanations.

Bynner, Witter: THE WAY OF LIFE ACCORDING TO LAOTZU
New York, Day 1944.
An American version, which is also its subtitle. It's based on English versions of that time. In the effort to clarify the chapters, he allows himself to deviate quite far from Lao Tzu's text.

Chen, Ellen M.: THE TAO TE CHING
New York, Paragon 1989.
With a knowledge that is only surpassed by the categorical attitude, Chen presents a version that includes but is far from dominated by the Mawangdui manuscripts. Lots of facts are also included, as well as far-reaching personal interpretations of Taoist philosophy and how to apply it.

Cheng, Man-jan: LAO TZU: MY WORDS ARE VERY EASY TO UNDERSTAND
California, North Atlantic Books 1981. Translated to English by Tam C. Gibbs.
Cheng comments the chapters of the text in short lessons, focused on the principles of Taoism. The explanations are so short that they don't add much to the text itself. The Chinese text is included in the book.

Cleary, Thomas: THE ESSENTIAL TAO
San Francisco, Harper Collins 1993.

The East Asian Studies PhD has translated several Taoist and Buddhist texts, which have been published in a number of different volumes. This one contains the texts of both Lao Tzu and Chuang Tzu. His translation is competent, although his choice of words is sometimes odd, deviating from the usual solutions.

Crowley, Aleister: THE TAO TEH KING
1918. Several editions in print.
The famous occultist made his own very personal interpretation of the text, where the hexagrams of *I Ching* have also been used. Crowley is always worth reading, although it's not certain that he speaks according to the Tao of Lao Tzu.

Duyvendak, J.J.L.: TAO TE CHING
London, Murray 1954.
This professor in Chinese fills his version of the text with elaborate comments, including linguistic and philosophical aspects. This version is one of the few that met the approval of the prominent sinologist Bernhard Karlgren.

Feng, Gia-fu & English, Jane: LAO TSU: TAO TE CHING
London, Wildwood 1973.
This version is simple and rewarding, although it isn't always in accordance with prevalent opinion. It lacks commentaries, but is richly illustrated with both calligraphy of the chapters and mood-filled photographs.

Henricks, Robert: TE-TAO CHING
New York, Ballantine 1989.
The professor of religion manages a very trustworthy version of the text, based primarily on the manuscripts of Ma-

wangdui. Because of their order, he has reversed the words of the title. His comments are knowledgeable and precise. The Mawangdui texts in Chinese are also included. This is a major work on the Mawangdui findings.

Henricks, Robert: LAO TZU'S TAO TE CHING
New York, Columbia University Press 2000.
In this book, Henricks concentrates on the findings in Guodian, which are competently presented and examined. They are also compared to the Mawangdui and Wang Pi versions. The texts are included in Chinese. The problem with the book is that the order of the chapters is according to the findings, which makes it difficult to use as a reference. Hopefully, Henricks finds a solution for it in a coming edition.

Ivanhoe, Philip J.: THE DAODEJING OF LAOZI
Indianapolis, Hackett 2002.
The historian of Chinese thought has made a straightforward and clean translation of the text, a learned introduction to it, and comparisons between other translations. There are also many informative notes.

Jiyu, Ren: A TAOIST CLASSIC: THE BOOK OF LAO ZI
Beijing, Foreign Languages Press 1993.
This Chinese version translated to English also contains precise explanations that focus on how to understand the philosophy of the text and of Taoism. The interpretation and the perspectives are frequently quite far from those of most Western translators, which makes the book particularly interesting to study.

Julien, Stanislas: LE LIVRE DE LA VOIE ET DE LA VERTU
Paris 1842.
Julien was a professor in Chinese at the Paris University. His French version is the first printed one in a Western language. It is still in print, as a facsimile. Unfortunately, no English translation of it seems to be in print.

Karlgren, Bernhard: NOTES ON LAO-TSE
Bulletin of Östasiatiska Museet, nr. 47/1975. Offprint.
The world famous Swedish sinologist finally published, just three years before his demise, a version of the text. He did so in a way as modest as was his habit – in a magazine of the Stockholm East Asian Museum. His interpretation is precise and clarifying, but the comments are minimal. At the time of his interpretation, the findings in Mawangdui were not at his disposal.

Lau, D.C.: LAO TZU: TAO TE CHING
London, Penguin 1963.
This professor of Chinese literature gives a knowledgeable and clear interpretation of the text. The book also contains explicit comments and explanations. In later editions of this book, Lau includes the findings in Mawangdui and Guodian.

Legge, James: THE TAO TEH KING
London, Oxford 1891.
Legge's historically significant version has extensive explanations with many references to the Chinese pictograms and their meaning. Still, his translation is aged, especially because of its effort to create poetry, which makes it deviate considerably from the wording of the original.

道德經

Le Guin, Ursula K., and Seaton, J. P.: LAO TZU: TAO TE CHING
Boston, Shambhala 1997.
The famous fantasy and science fiction writer has made an elegant and very clear version of the text, in collaboration with a professor of Chinese. There are some comments, especially on how the chapters should be understood and on some linguistic aspects.

Mair, Victor H.: TAO TE CHING
New York, Bantam 1990.
This professor of Chinese bases his interpretation on the Mawangdui manuscripts. The books also contains extensive comments, especially those comparing the text with the ideas of ancient India.

Maurer, Herrymon: TAO: THE WAY OF THE WAYS
England, Wildwood 1986.
These interpretations and comments are aimed at explaining the text's spiritual content, which is done quite cryptically at times. In spite of the late date of this version, Maurer is unfamiliar with the Mawangdui manuscripts.

Mitchell, Stephen: TAO TE CHING: A NEW ENGLISH VERSION
USA, Harper & Row 1988.
This version, with very limited comments, seems to be made without noticeable knowledge of the Mawangdui manuscripts. Still, it has its merits as a simple and direct interpretation of the text. Later editions have made it to the bestseller lists.

Ryden, Edmund: LAOZI: DAODEJING
Oxford University Press 2008.
This version includes the Mawangdui and Guodian findings. The introduction and comments are learned, but the wording in the translation sometimes gives the impression of being dated. Ryden translates *Te* as "the life force," which is similar to Arthur Waley's choice of "the power."

Star, Jonathan: TAO TE CHING
New York, Tarcher Penguin 2001.
The subtitle says that this is the definitive edition, which can be discussed. But its material is very rich. The interpretation of the text is given in Star's own words, but also word by word parallel to the Chinese signs – completely according to the Wang Pi version. There is also some other valuable material in the book. It is quite useful to the devoted student of the *Tao Te Ching*. In spite of its late publishing date, the Guodian manuscript seems unknown to the author. That might be corrected in later editions.

Ta-Kao, Chu: TAO TE CHING
London, Mandala 1959.
Ta-Kao allows himself to rearrange the text according to what he feels is the most probable. That can be discussed. Otherwise, his interpretation is straightforward and clear. The comments are sparse.

Wagner, Rudolf G.: A CHINESE READING OF THE DAODEJING
Albany, State University of New York Press 2003.
This is a translation of the Wang Pi commented version of the *Tao Te Ching*, which is the most cherished one in Chinese

literature, a classic in its own right. The translation is very competently done, and so are the expert comments. The Chinese text is included. A must for the study of Wang Pi as well as Lao Tzu, but not an easy book to digest.

Waley, Arthur: THE WAY AND ITS POWER
London, Unwin 1934.
Waley's cherished version is assisted by elaborate comments and a long introduction. His interpretations of the chapters are not always the most probable, but his book has won the respect of several important sinologists.

Wilhelm, Richard: TAO TE CHING
London, Arkana 1985. Translated by H.G. Ostwald.
The first edition of Wilhelm's important interpretation in German was published in 1910. In later editions it was reworked considerably. The comments from 1925 are elaborate about both the language aspects and the ideas of the text. Wilhelm also made a widely spread version of the *I Ching*, where he had C. G. Jung write the foreword. It's a pity he didn't do the same with the *Tao Te Ching*.

Wing, R. L.: THE TAO OF POWER
New York, Doubleday 1986.
This version includes the Chinese writing, also calligraphy as well as other illustrations of interest. The writer has allowed himself the freedom of adapting some of the wordings to modern concepts. The findings in Mawangdui seem not to be used at all.

Yutang, Lin: THE WISDOM OF LAOTSE
New York, Random 1948.

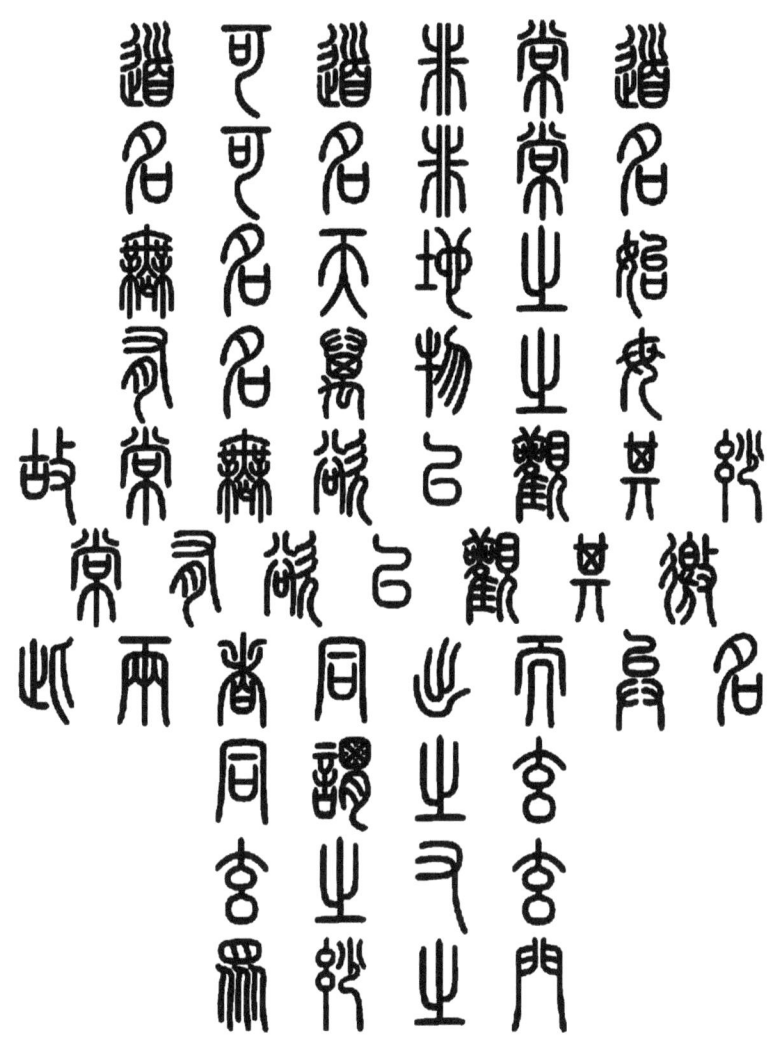

Seal script version of the first chapter of the Tao Te Ching.

The famous Chinese author made a pleasant interpretation, bordering on religious devotion. The book also contains a quantity of comments and explanations.

道德經

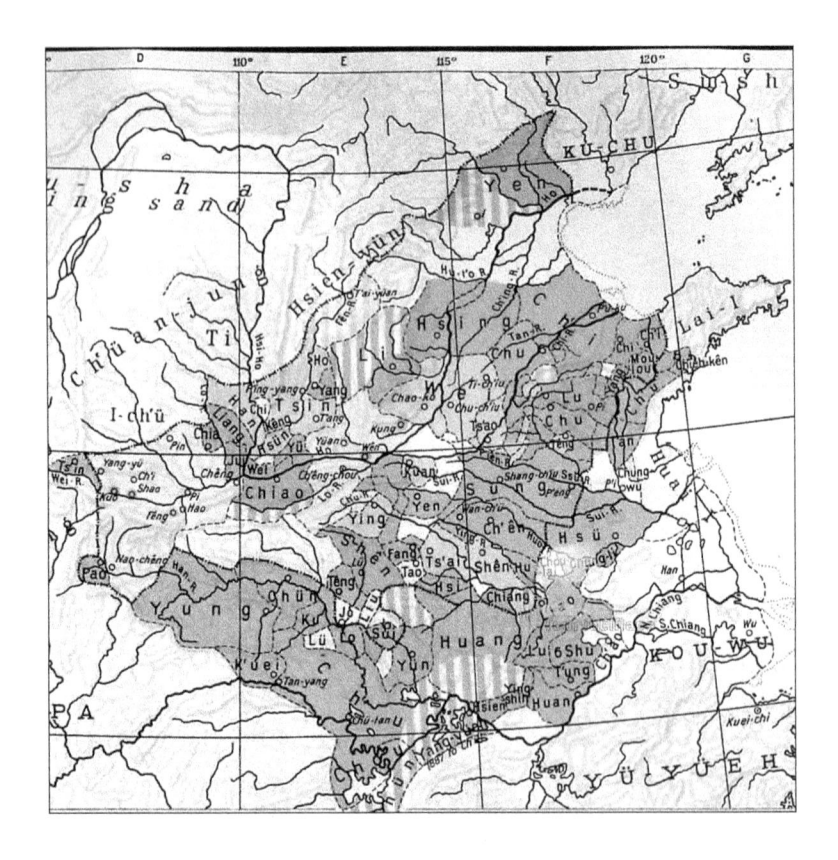

Map of China during the Chou (Zhou) Dynasty, c. 1045-221 BC. The dating of the Chinese Dynasties differs slightly from source to source, and time to time. The time of Lao Tzu was either late in the Spring and Autumn Period, c. 722-481 BC, or early in the Warring States Period, c. 480-221 BC.